Masterworks from The Museum of the American Indian
HEYE FOUNDATION

Introduction by Frederick J. Dockstader

THE METROPOLITAN MUSEUM OF ART

Masterworks from the Museum of the American Indian

AN EXHIBITION AT THE METROPOLITAN MUSEUM OF ART

OCTOBER 18 TO DECEMBER 31, 1973

Front and back covers
Navajo Woman
by R. C. Gorman, 1973
Catalogue number 200

Frontispiece
El Pensador Effigy
Buena Vista, Colima, Mexico. 100 B.C.–250 A.D.
Catalogue number 36

Composition by York Typesetting Co. Inc.
Printed by The Meriden Gravure Company
Designed by Sophie Adler

Library of Congress Cataloging in Publication Data

New York (City). Museum of the American Indian,
  Heye Foundation.
  Masterworks from the Museum of the American
Indian, Heye Foundation.

  Catalog of an exhibition held at the Metropolitan
Museum of Art, New York.
  Bibliography: p.
  1. Indians—Art—Exhibitions. 2. New York (City).
Museum of the American Indian, Heye Foundation.
I. New York (City). Metropolitan Museum of Art.
II. Title.
E59.A7N46   1973   709'.01'109701   73-16378
ISBN 0-87099-082-9

Masterworks from
The Museum of
The American Indian

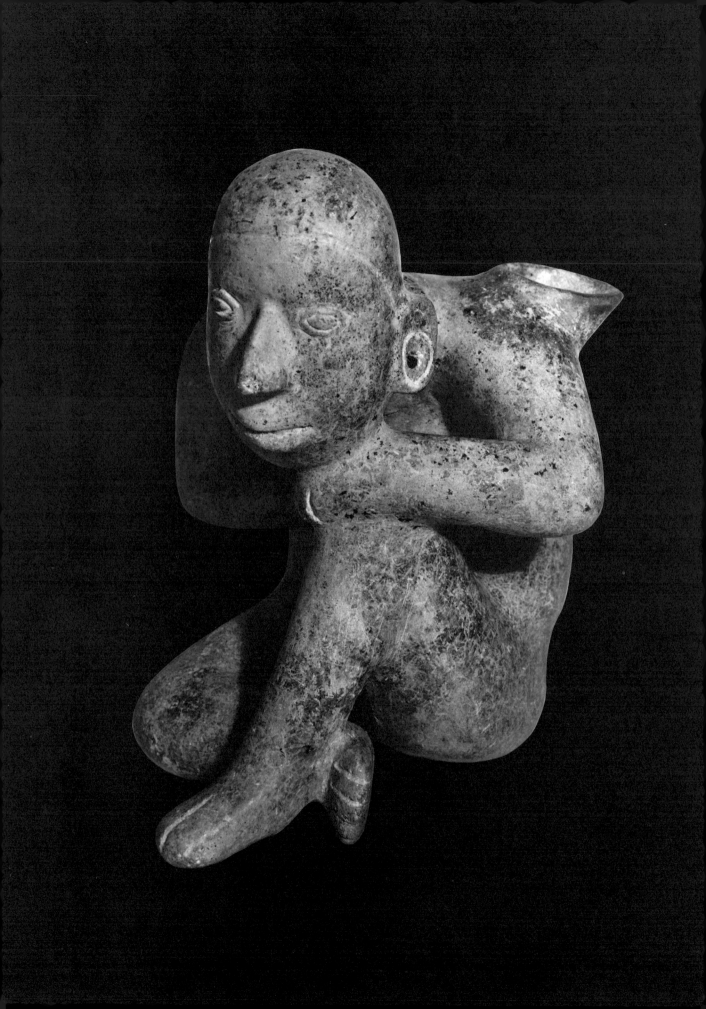

Prefatory Statements

For more than a century the Metropolitan Museum has borrowed important objects from institutions all over the world. In the present instance we have stayed close to home and mounted an entire exhibition from the holdings of a sister institution right here in New York, the Museum of the American Indian, Heye Foundation. We are delighted that the Museum and its Director, Frederick J. Dockstader, have let us show a selection of masterpieces from its collections – and the occasion is doubly pleasureful for both institutions in that we are able to make the opening of the exhibition a benefit for the American Association of Museums. It is a further deep pleasure for me to thank the National Endowment for the Arts and Philip Morris Incorporated on behalf of Marlboro for their financial sponsorship of these significant events.

Thomas Hoving
Director
The Metropolitan Museum of Art

This exhibition of masterpieces was selected from the vast collections of the Museum of the American Indian, Heye Foundation. It reflects the rich cultural heritage of all the varied and mysterious Indian civilizations that extended down the American continents from the Arctic to Tierra del Fuego. And it offers what we feel is an unprecedented opportunity to compare and contrast, in one place and at one time, the esthetic achievements of Amerindian societies as they have evolved over the last 4,000 years.

We are proud to sponsor such a showing, and intrigued, of course, by the Indian reverence for tobacco. "As soon as tobacco became known," writes the great French anthropologist, Claude Lévi-Strauss, in his studies of the myths of the South American Indians, "it combined with honey to form a pair endowed with supreme virtues."

By bringing you this rich assemblage we desire that you share with us a deeply felt, almost tangible presence of Indian thinking and feeling—of a vital way of life that can only be evoked through these extraordinary Indian images.

George Weissman
Vice-Chairman
Philip Morris Incorporated

For this highly important and timely exhibition we are in-debted to the Museum of the American Indian, Heye Foundation. From its collections the Director, Frederick J. Dockstader, and his staff have made a brilliant selection of masterpieces which present a vivid and inspiring over-all view of the artistic accomplishments of the Indian peoples of the Americas from ancient times to the present.

The American Association of Museums will benefit from the gala opening night at the Metropolitan. Thus, to the staff of that Museum, and to its Director, Thomas Hoving, we owe grateful thanks for this generosity in assisting the Association in its work of representing more than 1300 museums of science, history, and art on a national level. We are particularly grateful to The National Endowment for the Arts and to Philip Morris Incorporated for the financial assistance which has made this project possible.

On behalf of the American Association of Museums I also express appreciation to Mrs. Rodman Rockefeller and to His Excellency, Don Fernando Berckemeyer, Ambassador to the United States from Peru; His Excellency, the Ambassador of Mexico, Dr. José Juan de Olliqui; His Excellency, the Ambassador of Canada, Marcel Cadieux; and His Excellency, the Ambassador of Nicaragua, Dr. Guillermo Sevilla-Sacasa, as co-chairmen for the Metropolitan benefit evening.

Charles E. Buckley
President
American Association of Museums

Introduction

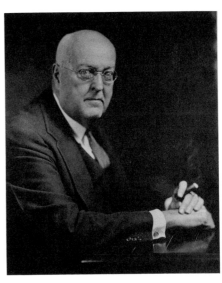

Dr. George G. Heye

This exhibition, drawn entirely from the collections of the Museum of the American Indian, owes its existence to the devoted efforts of Dr. George G. Heye. For approximately sixty years he invested his time and his money in building what is today the largest collection of native American material in the world.

Born in New York City, September 16, 1874, Heye was the son of Frederick Gustav and Marie Antoinette Lawrence Heye. The father, a businessman in Oil City, Pennsylvania, made his fortune with the Standard Oil Company. Young George graduated from the School of Mines, Columbia University, in 1896 with a degree in electrical engineering, and he began his career as a bridge-builder. While supervising the construction of a railroad bridge in Kingman, Arizona, in 1896, he encountered his first Indian – a Navajo laborer – from whom he purchased a buckskin shirt. This was the start of the Heye Collection.

The young man continued to collect, adding objects in an irregular fashion. In 1899 he participated in his first field trip, visiting the Cattaraugus Reservation in New York with Joseph Keppler, the owner of a major Indian collection. The same year, Heye met Marshall H. Saville and George H. Pepper, archeologists attached to the American Museum of Natural History. These men were influential in focusing Heye's interest on the study of American Indian material culture. Acting on the advice of Pepper, Heye purchased his first large collection in 1903 – archeological objects from New Mexico. After this, his course was set. During the next few years he sponsored or participated in several expeditions, including the Marie A. Heye Expedition (named after his mother) to Ecuador in 1906, the Samuel A. Barrett Expedition to the Cayapa in 1908-09, an archeological expedition in California, and extensive explorations in the West Indies. Well-known professionals took part in all these ventures, and today their findings are still significant. Indeed, some represent the only surviving evidence we have from particular prehistoric sites.

By 1915 Heye's collections were large enough for them to become known as The Heye Museum, and he gratefully accepted Archer M. Huntington's offer of land for a building at Audubon Terrace – a location on upper Broadway that placed his efforts in proximity with several other specialized institutions. (It was then felt that Audubon Terrace would ultimately

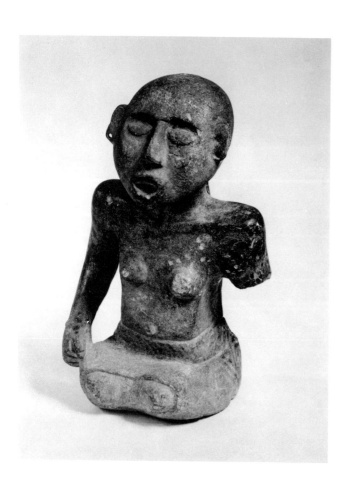

18 Female Effigy
Tumlin Mound. Bartow County, Georgia
1200-1600. Height: 15½ inches   14/1455
Some figures like this were interred in stone-lined
crypts, others were apparently set up in temples.
They may have been idols, ancestral figures, or
memorials to individuals of the community.

become a cultural center for New York City.) The Museum of the American Indian, Heye Foundation, was founded May 10, 1916. Continued expansions of the collections made it necessary to add a storage building in the Bronx. Later, the Museum's splendid James B. Ford Library was established in space provided by the Huntington Free Library and Reading Room.

The decade following the end of World War I was the Museum's Golden Age. The rate of collecting increased greatly, and the staff grew in number and importance to include most of the outstanding anthropologists of the period. Frank G. Speck, Samuel K. Lothrop, T. T. Waterman, Alanson Skinner, Melvin R. Gilmore, and Mark R. Harrington – to name only a few – not only collected as professional field workers on behalf of the Museum but also undertook field studies, expeditions, and excavations. Edward H. Davis worked for the Museum among the Indians of California and northern Mexico, Donald A. Cadzow collected Cree material in Alberta, and A. Hyatt Verrill worked in Central and South America. Each of these specialists brought back large amounts of material as well as field notes and photographs, and these were subsequently published. The excavation at Háwikuh, the first Zuni village encountered by Coronado in 1540, was one of the Museum's major efforts, and even today it ranks as one of the largest archeological efforts ever carried out in the Southwest. The backer of this venture of 1917-23, known as the Hendricks-Hodge Expedition, was Harmon W. Hendricks, a retired business executive, and the leader was Frederick Webb Hodge, then the dean of American anthropologists. Dr. Heye himself was frequently in the field, and crates of new material arriving at the Museum were but one of the results. A productive hunting ground for Heye was Europe, where important Indian material had been sent or taken in the eighteenth and nineteenth centuries and even earlier.

It was when Dr. Hodge joined the staff that the Museum's publishing program entered its great period. The Museum's series, now totaling more than 400 titles, includes some of the most important studies yet made of the Indian. The program is still active, and new monographs are issued regularly.

In addition to Archer Huntington and Harmon Hendricks, James B. Ford, Minor C. Keith, and Blair S. Williams – all of these men serving as trustees of the Museum – helped Heye's vision to flourish. And Thea Kowne Page, whom Dr. Heye married in 1915, brought to the projects her own enthusiasm and the backing of her personal funds. Heye, though he lived until 1957, never fully recovered from the death of his wife in 1935.

112 Polychrome Urn
Tiahuanaco-Huari. Nazca, Peru, 750-1000
Height: 12½ x 10 inches   16/9700

Decorated with a design of a masked figure, zoömorphic figures, and geometric designs. Unusual for its size and excellent condition. Collected by George G. Heye.

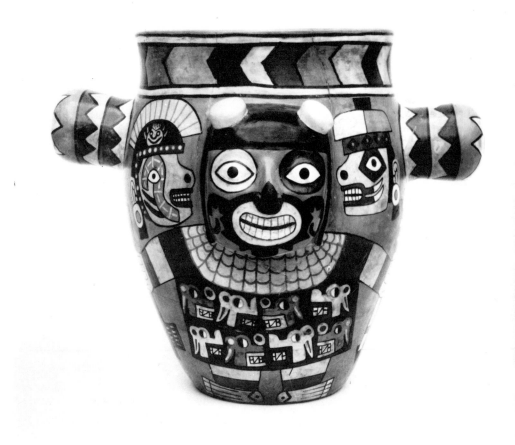

9

The Depression canceled many of the ambitious plans for the Museum that were under consideration at the beginning of the 1930s, particularly those regarding the storage building, known today as the Research Branch. It was once hoped that this location would become a showplace, exhibiting Indian gardens, foodstuffs, dwellings, and other out-of-door attractions, where the entire Indian world could be reviewed in microcosm. This grand design never matured.

Heye's primary desire was for his Museum to provide a complete picture of Indian life, and to this end a simple stirring stick was to him as significant in its own way as the most elaborately carved and painted totem pole – both were part of the heritage and development of the native American, as were the 4,000,000 other objects in the collections, large or small, esthetic masterpiece (as in the present exhibition) or utilitarian tool. Heye's devotion to this single principle was recognized in part in 1929 when the University of Hamburg awarded him an honorary Ph.D. degree.

Heye had an exceptional memory, and toward the end of his life he could still recall the physical characteristics of most of the objects he had collected over the years. Perhaps the easiest single indication of his wholehearted concern is the fact that he personally catalogued every specimen, even to lettering the number. Thus, until his retirement, he physically handled every item in his collection, a distinction few, if any, of the other great collectors of the period could boast. Surprisingly, in view of his passion for large-scale efforts, Heye was not interested in personal publicity and remained little known to the outside world. He was not a writer, although there are a half-dozen titles to his credit; he was an active, rather than an analytic or introspective, individual.

After about 1950 he ceased to actively collect, and during the next few years the collection was administered by his friend and successor, Edwin K. Burnett. Burnett had been with the Museum approximately thirty years, and he knew the objects intimately. With Burnett's retirement in 1960, the transition from one-man museum was completed. However, the subsequent modernizations of the institution, administrative and other, have not affected the tradition as established by the founder: to collect what is Indian and to exclude what is not. There are no Remington or Russell or Catlin paintings in the collection; there are paintings by Awa Tsireh, Kabotie, and Tsatoke.

Because the collection as a whole is so vast, it is not easy for an outsider to know it properly. Its Clarence B. Moore Collection of Southeastern Archeology is perhaps the best known of the major components, but quite as deserving is the Northwest Coast Collection, largely the work of Lt. George T. Emmons, the Marshall H. Saville Collections from South America, the field work of Samuel K. Lothrop in Middle America, Edward H. Davis' work among the California peoples, and the field explorations of Mark R. Harrington. It is the *variety* of the information in these and the other components that makes the Museum so important. There are better holdings of Peruvian archeology in Peru and Mexican material in Mexico, and other specialized collections here and there may surpass the Heye efforts, but no other collection possesses the comprehensive representation that is so helpful, ultimately, to the scholar.

If there is a serious shortcoming in the breadth of the collection, it would be in the contemporary field. The wealth of tribal representation tapers off rather sharply after about 1940. This is accounted for by the laws of time and economics. Earlier, it was imperative to salvage material that was rapidly disappearing; later, with prices soaring on more recent productions and the number of significant producers ever decreasing, and with the advent of new museums and collectors in the Indian areas, acquisition inevitably had to decline. This is not necessarily an undesirable development, since it signals a healthy increase of interest in Indian crafts production. The Museum feels that some of this interest, at least, has come from its efforts to awaken people to the values inherent in Indian culture.

The recent expansion of the Museum's activities has been directed toward the educational and cultural needs of the

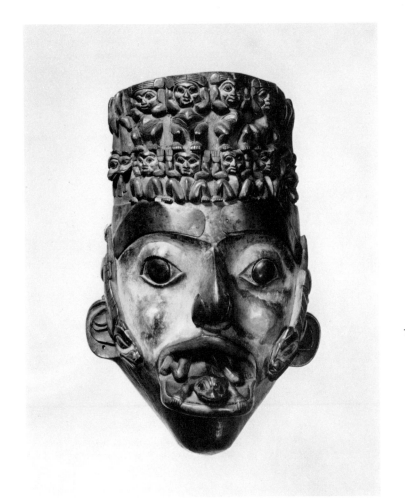

132 Otter Woman Mask
Tlingit. Gaudekan, Alaska, 1825-1850
Height: 13 inches   9/7989

Represents the spirit of an old woman with a frog emerging from her mouth. On either cheek is an otter, while land spirits decorate the band across the forehead. The eyes are inlaid with Russian trade buttons; the brows are of sheet copper. Collected by G. T. Emmons.

public. The increasing demands of the Indian peoples for civil, legal, and social justice have aroused the Museum's concern – how could they fail to? – yet the Museum, as chartered, must remain a nonpolitical institution. It has elected to serve the developing needs by aggressively demonstrating the dignity and talent inherent in the native American culture, and by promoting these values in every way possible. A much more relaxed loan policy (Dr. Heye was reluctant to lend) has allowed the Museum to share its objects with schools, colleges, and museums throughout the country. The present exhibition is an example of these efforts. In bringing some of the esthetic triumphs of the native American before a new audience at the Metropolitan Museum, we feel we are exercising our responsibility not only to the collection Dr. Heye built but also to those great civilizations that were here ahead of the Europeans and which continue, albeit in greatly modified form, to the present time. We regard this exhibition as a tribute to those artists who first came to America and added their beauty to Nature's own wonders.

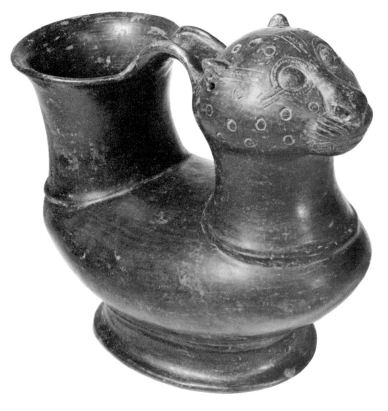

97 Jaguar Effigy Vessel
Tairona. Fundación, Colombia
1200-1600
9 x 10 inches   22/7106

Of polished blackware. Presented by Emma Olin, Minerva Olin Edwurm, and Ernest A. Olin.

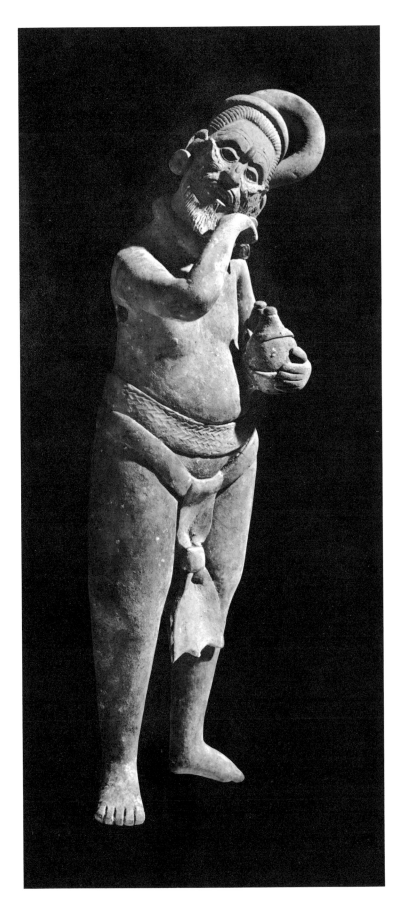

65 Standing Figurine
Maya. Jaina Island, Mexico, 550-900
Height: 14¹/₂ inches   23/2573

An unusually large example, this pensive
ceramic figure, sensitively modeled, holds
two clay vessels in his left arm.

13

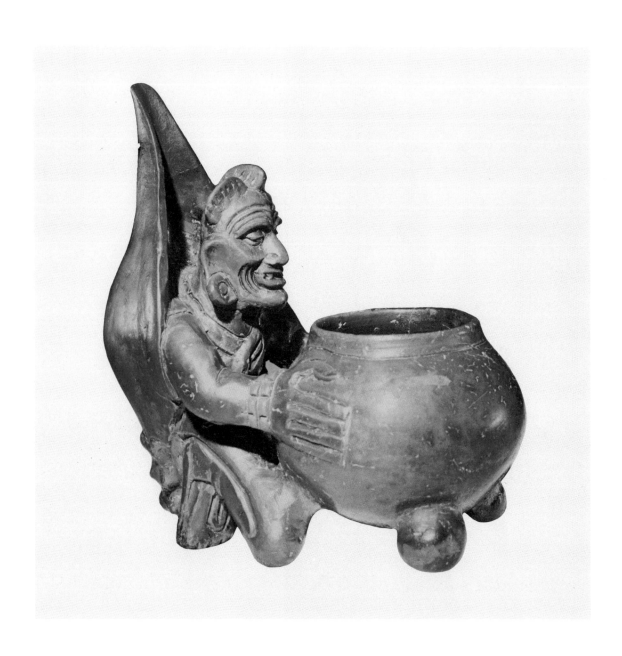

69 Plumbate Effigy Vessel
Maya. Guaymil, Mexico, 900-1200
9 x 9½ inches   23/900

This effigy of the Fire God seated in the heart of
a conch shell, and holding an offering bowl in his
lap, is a unique combination of forms. The Fire
God is a whistle, the conch shell can be blown
as a trumpet, and pebbles in the legs make it into
a rattle. Presented by Major Marion Eppley.

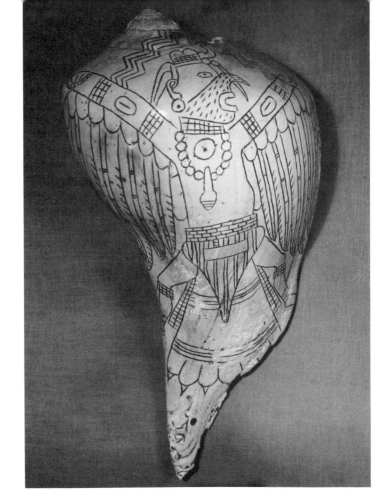

15 Incised Conch Shell
Spiro Mound. LeFlore County, Oklahoma
1200-1600. Length: 13 inches   18/9121

The designs on the Spiro Mound conch shells frequently show how the objects were used. Presumably this depicts a ceremonial dancer, the Eagle Man. Presented by Mrs. James B. Clemens.

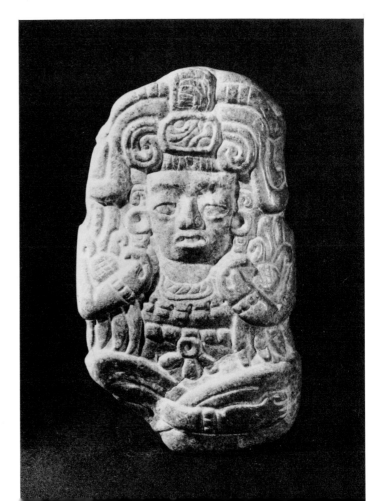

58 Carved Jade
Maya. Copán, Honduras, 550-950
4¹/₄ x 7³/₄ inches   10/9827

This representation of a seated Mayan dignitary is of unusually large size. Weighing more than five pounds, it could hardly have been worn as an adornment. Collected in 1915 by Thomas Gann, presented by Archer M. Huntington.

The first immigrants came to the New World approximately 40,000 years ago, crossing from Asia via the Bering Strait, and they continued to come this way until some 5,000 years before the arrival of the first Europeans. It may well be that additional populations developed in South America from the landings of transpacific voyagers, but even the few reasonably safe speculations about this dimly known initial period are too many to discuss here. What really matters in our context is that major cultural triumphs, non-European in origin, were ultimately to be found throughout the Americas. As the objects in the exhibition attest, the Indian civilizations developed independently and generally at great distances from one another. Could one have made a "Cook's Tour" from British Columbia south into Mexico and Costa Rica, and thence on into Ecuador and Peru during the period 1250-1500 A.D., astonishingly advanced civilizations would have been encountered. This same trip, taken a thousand years earlier, would have been less rewarding – and taken in 1850, it would have been a depressing experience indeed. Thus, in simplest curve, we run the graphline of Indian history. The rest of the story, insofar as we are concerned with it here, can be suggested by brief reminders of some of the many materials used by the Indian creators.

The permanence of fired clay makes pottery the best known of the numerous survivors of prehistoric cultures. The oldest object in the exhibition comes from Valdivia in Ecuador, the site where pottery apparently first developed in the New World. The Indians became remarkably skilled in forming magnificent objects from clay, and scholars still wonder how some of the great burial urns were fired. Some of the elaborate effigies impress us profoundly as technical achievements long before we consider their esthetic merits.

Shell was an equally popular basic material, worked in innumerable ways in many places. While we will never know the full extent of this usage – much of the fragile substance having vanished through the action of acidic soils – we have ancient shell trumpets, bells and ornaments, beads, buttons, and inlays. The artists' obvious fascination with colors, delicacy, and ease of crafting of shell was heightened by their sense of its importance in relation to water. They frequently went to great trouble to obtain the material, sometimes going on overland trading journeys of thousands of miles to reach the source of supply.

The Indians, as is well known, carved a great variety of stones: nephrite, jade, serpentine, carnelian, quartz, diorite, basalt, and alabaster were all favored, especially for smaller works. Scoria, tufa, and other volcanic stone were used for larger works. Turquoise was sought after as a setting, as were lapis lazuli and agate.

Indian metalwork encompassed copper, gold, and even platinum. Silver was the least used of the metals in ancient times, and iron was also rarely worked. The working of gold, which began quite early, became surprisingly widespread.

Archeologically speaking, wood is rare throughout the New

106 Gold Crown

Coastal Chavín. Chongoyape, Peru
900-500 B.C.
5½ x 9½ inches   16/1972B

An example of Coastal Chavín goldsmith's art, the earliest gold work yet
known in the Americas. This richly
embossed crown was probably worn
with a textile band wrapped around
the plain base to hold it firmly on
the head.

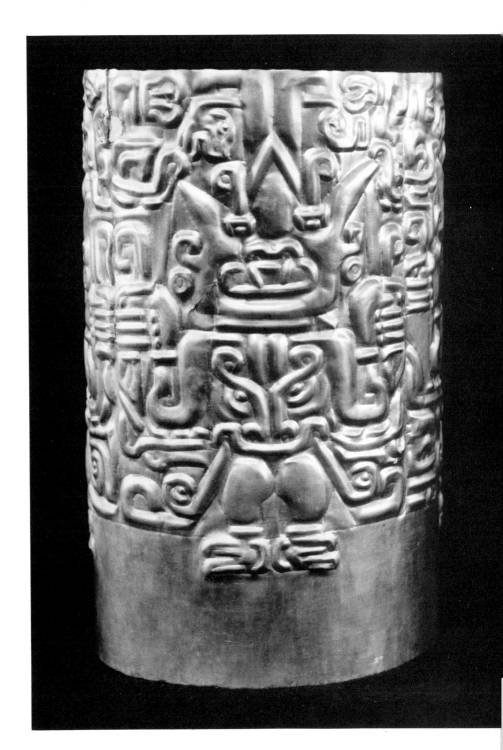

World; it has survived only in the relatively dry desert areas or in an occasional cave. The *atlatl* shaft from Mexico is a rarity as well as a legacy of a widespread artistry.

The Northwest Coast Indians were the master carvers of North America, equaled only, in the opinion of some, by the Maya. Great stands of timber made wood the natural medium for the Northwest Coast artists, and from it they produced their masks and totem poles. These works were carefully and intricately carved, and many of them were brilliantly inlaid with shell.

Aside from wood, superb carving in the Northwest Coast region was done in ivory (obtained from the walrus and whale) or bone. This material assumed a beautiful patina after being polished through years of use, giving the pieces – "soul catchers" and shamans' charms – an added importance in Indian eyes. The peoples of Mexico and Peru had a similar fondness for bone as a medium. Its tubular form led artists in many places to use it for musical instruments – whistles, flutes – and costume ornaments. Horn, another animal substance, offered ease of working. After boiling or other heating, it would be worked into spoons, ladles, or other flattened-out objects, and it was suited for carving and inlaying.

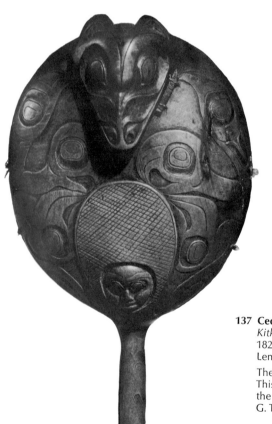

137 Cedar Wood Rattle
Kitksan. Skeena River, British Columbia
1825-1875
Length: 11½ inches   9/7998

The round type of rattle is used only by shamans. This example is carved to represent the beaver; the hatched area depicts the tail. Collected by G. T. Emmons.

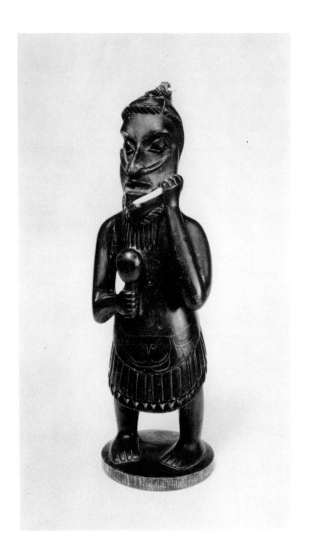

145 Carved Figurine
Haida. Queen Charlotte Islands
British Columbia, circa 1850
Height: 18½ inches   23/701

This effigy of a standing shaman is made of
cedar with ivory ornaments added. From a 19th-
century English collection, presented by Major
Marion Eppley.

The Indians' mastery of weaving and the related textile
crafts, including dyeing, can leave no modern observer un-
impressed. The work of the Peruvians in vicuña, llama, and
alpaca wools was of an unparalleled fineness, and many of
the pieces that have come down to us are as striking in their
brilliant colors and designs as when they were originally
produced.

Today, the major centers of Indian weaving are in Ecuador
and Peru, Guatemala and Mexico, Arizona and New Mexico.
The artists in each of these regions have maintained, if not
really increased, the technical skills and artistic designing of
their ancestors, so that the best of the living Maya and Navajo
weavers can hold their own in competition with any weavers
elsewhere in the world.

The early inhabitants of all regions made fine baskets, and
the craft traditions have long endured. The splendid basketry
of the Pomo people is no less impressive, technically and
artistically, than the work one encounters in the oldest Peruvian textiles.

19

Not enough Indian painting has survived for it to receive the degree of appreciation that the other arts have received. However, the painted textiles and fragments of painted wood that we have, as well as the decoration applied to some pottery after firing, prove that painting was not a minor art form. The painted conch shell is one very early example of painting. The art of painting on paper, so familiar to us today, existed in earlier times as work done on bark cloth, and was important even though its quantity was small. Today, Indian artists are seeking a new identification through painting, and many of them are torn between trying to maintain their quality of being Indian and at the same time trying to find a place in the world of modern art. This is a complicated situation, since the very treatment that identifies the artist's work as Indian defeats his hope of being recognized as an individual creator.

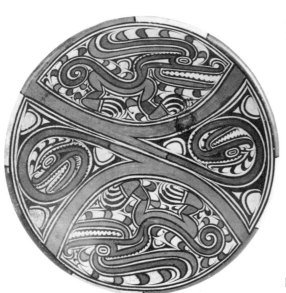

85 Polychrome Frutera
Veraguas. Río de Jesús, Panama
750-1250
Diameter: 13 inches   24/502

A complex design depicting a pair of Crocodile Gods and serpents. Excavated by Neville A. Harte, presented by Dr. and Mrs. Arthur M. Sackler.

The earlier Indian painter used animal hides, wood, or plaster walls as his canvas. While he created much awesome religious art, he also made images with humorous, satiric, irreverent, and even erotic connotations. Clearly, the early native was not, as some careless non-Indian thinking once had it, a rigidly serious person. Just as there can be no single Indian stereotype, there is no stereotype within his art: the expressions vary tremendously. While we can identify the expressions, as well as the media and techniques, as Indian, the variety is so great that the term "Indian art" needs always to be accompanied by notice of the given area, period, or tribe. Even so, each Indian form – as this exhibition amply demonstrates – has a richness, strength, and vitality that commands consideration for its own sake.

The exhibition presents a generally chronological approach to Indian culture. Since the objects are in no way intended to convey a balanced survey of the subject, a few liberties have been taken with archeological sequence and anthropological relationship. Some periods were more creative than others, some regions followed esthetic patterns more effectively than others. Occasionally, too, an example has been included for historic reasons, the rarity or other significance of the object perhaps outweighing its esthetic interest. It is our hope that the experience of viewing the exhibition may stimulate the visitor to explore the subject further, and to this end a bibliography has been appended.

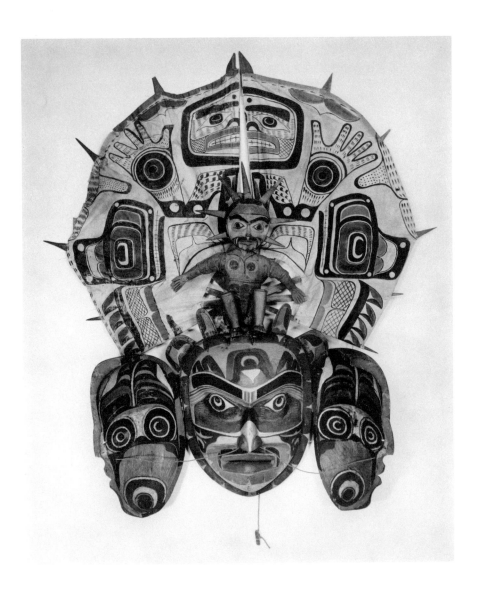

157 Mechanical Headdress

Kwakiutl. Alert Bay, British Columbia
1875-1900
46 x 52 inches   11/5235

Representing the sun and several spirits, this
carved and painted wooden mask has a painted
muslin backing. When the wearer pulls the
strings, the headdress expands and the mask
opens to reveal the inner spirit of the sun.
Collected by George G. Heye.

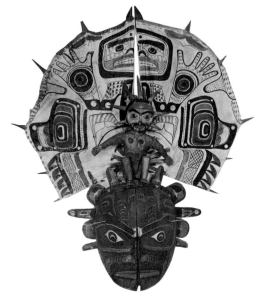

159 Wooden House Front

Nootka. Nootka Sound
British Columbia, circa 1875
67 x 109 inches   6/8700

Many Northwest Coast tribes painted designs on their wooden dwellings, employing animal motifs to identify and add prestige to the inhabitants. This example portrays the killer whale, bear, wolf, seal, and perhaps the owner himself in a linear pattern. Collected by D. F. Tozier.

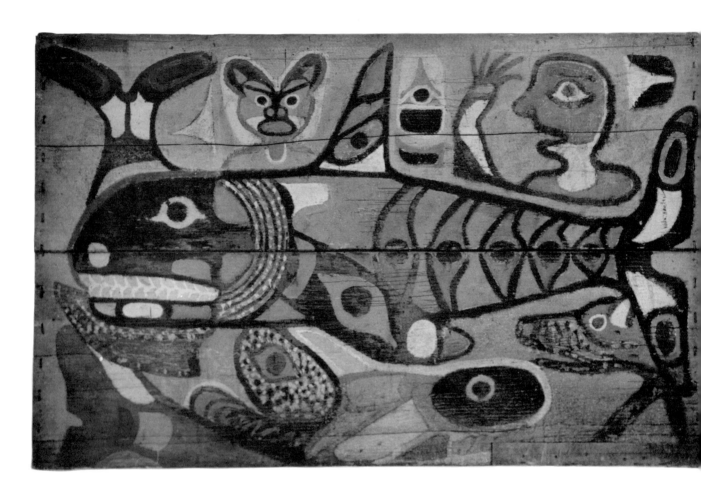

I acknowledge with pleasure the help of people who have made this exhibition possible. The discoverers and donors of the objects are credited in the captions to the illustrations. Lewis Krevolin, Lynette Miller, Marlene Martin, William Stiles, Anna Roosevelt, Vincent Wilcox, and Sophie Arctander – all of the staff of the Museum of the American Indian – were unstintingly generous with their time and talent, as were Douglas Newton, Bradford Kelleher, James Pilgrim, Karl Katz, and Lori Shepherd of the Metropolitan Museum.

John Spencer and Diane Kartalia of the National Endowment for the Arts were nobly helpful with their grant, as were George Weissman and Frank Saunders of Philip Morris. Their generosity, as extended through the genial aid of William Ruder and Caroline Goldsmith, has inspired all of us. For the photographs that so brilliantly illustrate this catalogue, we are proud of the skill of Carmelo Guadagno, staff photographer of the Museum, and his assistant, Carlos Castro-Rojas. And for keeping all of the details working smoothly, my thanks go to Stephanie Spivey. Finally, for the coordination of all this major effort, I acknowledge the help of Carla O'Rorke of this Museum, Jack Frizzelle of the Metropolitan, and Lee Kimche of the American Association of Museums.

Frederick J. Dockstader
Director
Museum of the American Indian

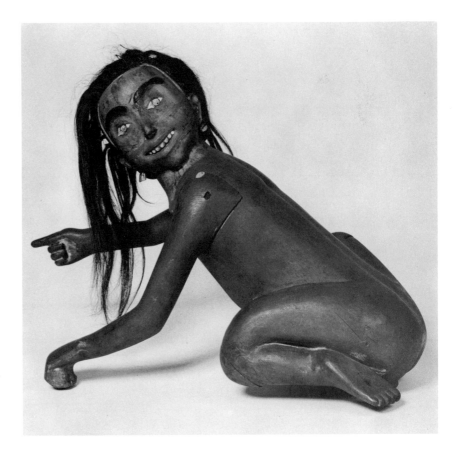

129 Canoe-Prow Effigy
Tlingit. Chilkat, Alaska, 1825-1875
14 x 21 inches   1/6713

Used on the prow to direct the canoe safely, this represents the Land Otter Man, a powerful being in Tlingit mythology, who rescues drowning people and transforms them into land otters. The sculpture is decorated with human hair, abalone-shell inlay, and opercula teeth. Collected by G. B. Gordon.

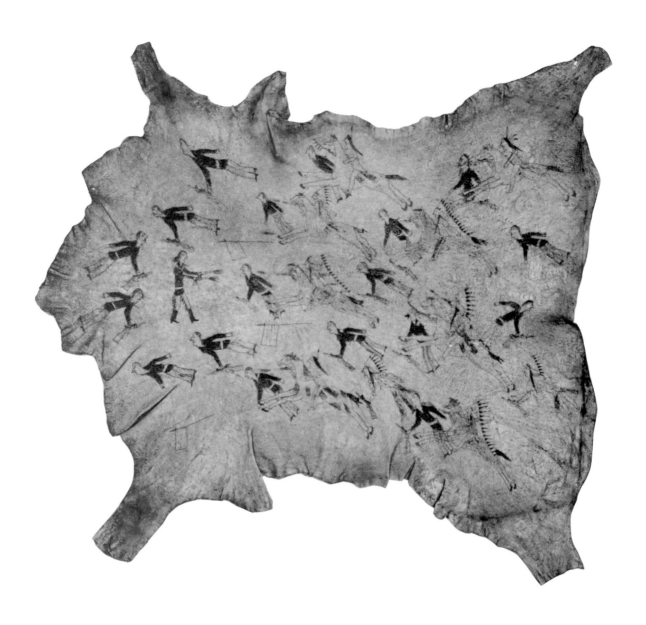

180 Painted Deer Hide

Cheyenne. Lame Deer, Montana, 1878
34 x 46 inches   18/4323

The scene is of the Battle of the Little
Bighorn; General Custer is at the left
center. The Cheyenne artist fought in
the battle. Collected by Frank Linabury.

The Exhibition

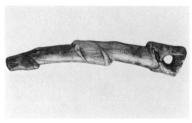

1

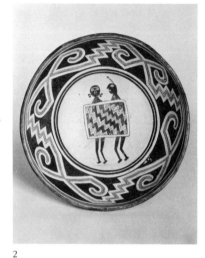

2

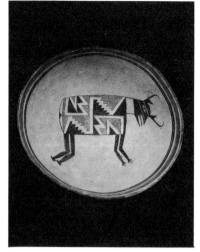

3

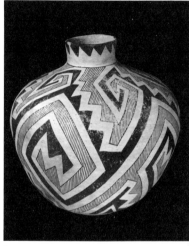

5

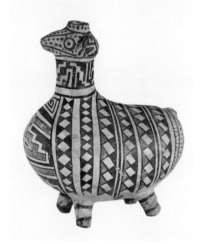

4

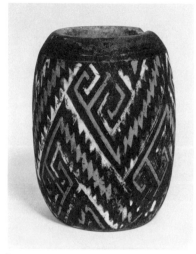

6

1 Adz Handle
Eskimo. Alaska, Old Bering Sea Culture
300 B.C.-300 A.D.
Length: 12¹/₂ inches   2/4318

Carved from fossil ivory, this at one
time had a jade or slate blade lashed to
the handle. The butt end is formed
into a wolf's head, and the handle is
composed of two walrus-head designs.
Collected by G. T. Emmons.

2 Black-on-White Bowl
Mimbres. New Mexico, 900-1100
Diameter: 10¹/₂ inches   24/3198

The Mimbres Valley region in south-
western New Mexico has yielded a
remarkable ceramic art. This design of
a young couple wrapped in a blanket
is an example of the human quality of
much of the ware. Presented by Dr.
and Mrs. Arthur M. Sackler.

3 Black-on-White Bowl
Mimbres. New Mexico, 900-1100
Diameter: 11 inches   24/3196

An example of the zoömorphic designs
found on the Mimbres ware, this
geometrically decorated antelope is
painted in a red brown (the result
of firing) on a white clay surface.
Presented by Dr. and Mrs. Arthur M.
Sackler.

4 Clay Effigy Vessel
Anasazi. Tularosa Canyon, New Mexico
1100-1300
8 x 9 inches   18/6406

Such figures are frequently found in
the Southwest. They were probably
used as magical charms or for quasi-
religious purposes. This vessel seems
to be an animal form.

5 Painted Sandstone Mortar
Pueblo Bonito. Chaco Canyon
New Mexico, circa 1200
Height: 8 inches   5/1364

With designs in red and green, this
mortar was excavated from Room 80 of
Pueblo Bonito—the largest prehistoric
site of its type in the Southwest—by
Dr. George H. Pepper. Presented by
Thea Heye.

6 Pottery Storage Vessel
Anasazi. Apache County, Arizona
1200-1500
10 x 12 inches   19/1820

A fine example of early Anasazi ware,
this *tinaja* was probably used for
carrying water. Collected by William
M. Fitzhugh.

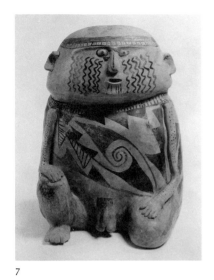

7

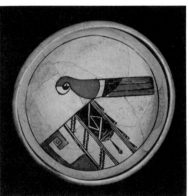

8

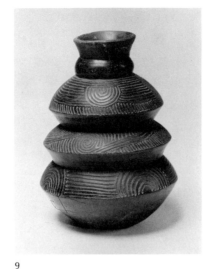

9

10

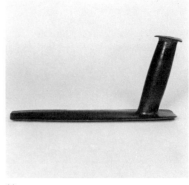

11

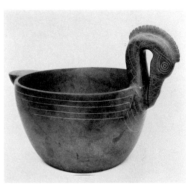

12

7 Large Effigy Vessel

Casas Grandes. Chihuahua, Mexico
1300-1500
Height: 13½ inches   24/3190

This unusually large polychrome
vessel, in the form of a kneeling nude
male figurine, represents a style that
at one time extended into the south-
western United States.

8 Polychrome Vessel

Háwikuh. New Mexico, 1400-1600
Diameter: 11 inches   8/6832

From the ancient Zuni village of
Háwikuh, one of the fabled Seven
Cities of Cíbola, visited by Coronado
in 1540. The site was excavated
between 1917 and 1923 by Frederick
Webb Hodge. Presented by Harmon
W. Hendricks.

9 Water Vessel

Caddoan. Carden Bottom, Arkansas
1200-1700
Height: 7 inches   5/6318

Of highly polished blackware, this
represents three bowls set on top of
one another. The incised scroll design
suggests a close relationship with
later Southeastern beadwork designs.
Collected by L. F. Branson.

10 Water Vessel

Caddoan. Ouachita Parish, Louisiana
1200-1700
Height: 5½ inches   17/3248

Another example of fine blackware
of the Southeast, reflecting the
predilection for scroll designs in clay.
Collected by Clarence B. Moore.

11 Steatite Monitor Pipe

Temple Mound II. Pulaski County
Virginia, 1200-1600
6¾ x 15 inches   18/2785

Such pipes, carefully crafted, were
used "as is," or were occasionally
smoked by inserting a small reed into
the shaft opening at the end. The
ancient artists' ability to work down a
boulder to this delicate form is a
measure of the technology of the
period. Presented by Henry L. Ferguson.

12 Crested Wood-Duck Bowl

Moundville. Hale County, Alabama
1200-1600
10 x 12 inches   16/5232

One of the great examples of prehistoric
North American art, this bowl is
carved from a single block of diorite.
Technically skillful, it also shows the
ability of the early artist to create
beauty from a simple form. Excavated
by Clarence B. Moore near Mound R
in 1905.

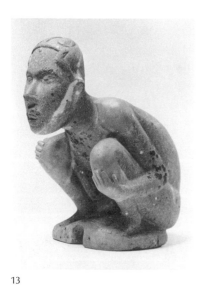

13

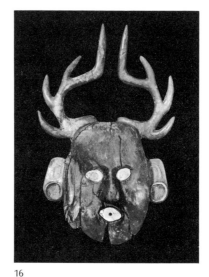

16

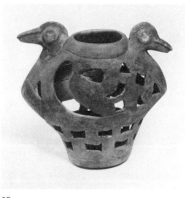

19

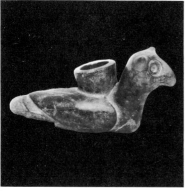

14

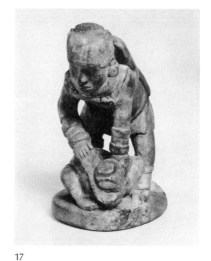

17

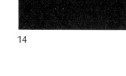

20

13 Sandstone Pipe

Moundville. Hale County, Alabama
1200-1600
4 x 8 inches   17/2810

The motif of a squatting man was common in the art of this period. Throughout most of North America tobacco had religious overtones, and elaborate pipes such as this were employed for ceremonial smoking. Excavated by Clarence B. Moore.

14 Steatite Pipe Bowl

East Laporte, North Carolina, 1200-1600
4 x 8¹/₂ inches   15/1085

Representing a horned owl, this is typical of many bird-form pipes used in the Temple Mound period. The eyes were originally inlaid. Collected by Charles O. Turbyfill.

15 Incised Conch Shell   (see page 15)

16 Deer-Man Mask

Spiro Mound. LeFlore County
Oklahoma, 1200-1600
7 x 11¹/₂ inches   18/9306

One of the very few old wooden masks that have survived. The surface was once painted, and the ears had shell inlays. Probably worn during the Deer Ceremony.

17 Warrior Pipe

Spiro Mound. LeFlore County
Oklahoma, 1200-1600
5 x 10 inches   21/4088

Apparently depicting the beheading of a victim by a warrior, the scene depicts customs common to the Southeast and Mesoamerica. Presented by The Viking Fund, Inc.

18 Female Effigy   (see page 8)

19 Openwork Vessel

Weeden Island. Washington County
Florida, 200-750
Height: 8¹/₂ inches   17/4875

An unusual form of ceramic ware found in Florida, the design enhanced with triangular cut-outs. Such vessels were presumably made simply for beauty's sake, rather than to function as containers. Collected by Clarence B. Moore.

20 Incised Shell Gorget

Temple Mound II. Sumner County
Tennessee, 1200-1600
Diameter: 4 inches   15/853

Such objects were worn on the breast, quite possibly as a form of insignia. This one, depicting a warrior apparently dancing with the head of his victim, has long been of interest to scholars studying Mexican influences on the pre-Columbian Southeast. Collected by W. E. Meyer.

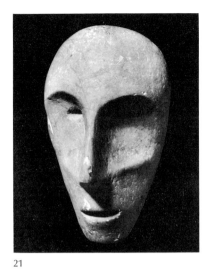

21

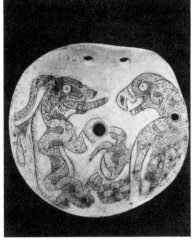

23

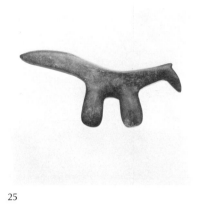

25

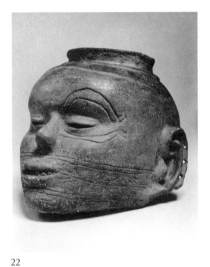

22

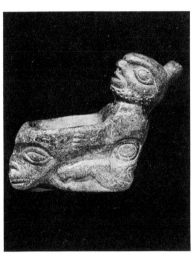

24

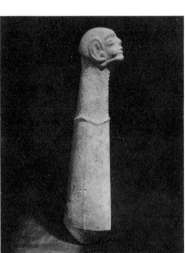

26

25 Stone "Slave Killer"
Dalles Culture. Gunther Island
Arcata Bay, California, 1000-1200
Length: 15 inches   23/1874

Despite the present-day name, such
implements may have had a wider
range of uses. The Harry H. Woodring
Collection.

26 Carved Stone Club
Dalles Culture. Buckley Canyon
British Columbia, 1200-1600
Length: 13 inches   12/3273

This may have been a ceremonial
baton, or it may have been intended
for use in warfare. The paddle-shaped
form is common in the region.

21 Stone Head
Temple Mound II. Gallatin County
Kentucky, 1200-1600
6 x 10 inches   6/397

Stone heads of this type, and others
carved even more realistically, are
known from many areas of the Southeast. The eyes of this example once
contained color. Presented by Thea
Heye.

22 Trophy Head Vessel
Temple Mound II. Blytheville, Arkansas
1200-1600
Height: 6 inches   5/2981

This may reflect the practice of taking
trophy heads in battle, or it may simply
represent the head of the person in
whose grave it was buried. Archeologists associate such vessels with the
"Southern Death Cult." Collected by
Thea Heye.

23 Shell Gorget
Temple Mound II. Bell County, Texas
1200-1500
Diameter: 5¹/₂ inches   22/7574

Made from a section of a huge conch
shell, this depicts a bear or a panther
confronting an eagle. It is surprising to
find such an example so far from the
boundaries of the Mississippian
Tradition. Collected by Dr. Alex Dienst.
Courtesy of Roger N. Conger.

24 Steatite Mortar
Dalles Culture. Washington, 1000-1200
Height: 7¹/₂ inches   1/9485

This is a form common in the Pacific
Northwest. Little is known of the
people inhabiting the region of The
Dalles; they may have been early Salish
Indians who spread throughout the
Northwest. Although found in Wash-
ington in 1870, the mortar more likely
originated in British Columbia.

29

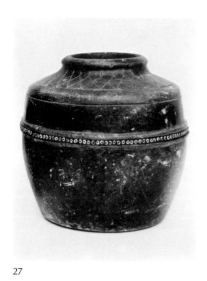

27

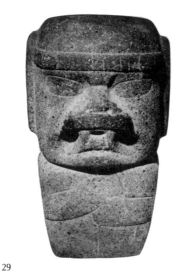

29

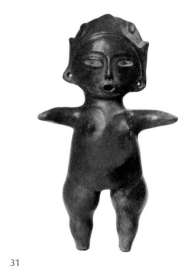

31

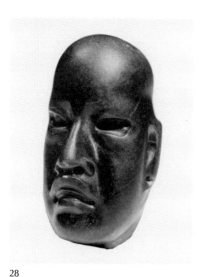

28

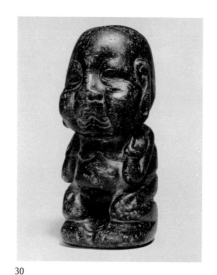

30

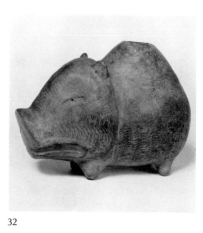

32

27 Steatite Mortar
Canaliño. Santa Catalina Island
California, 1400-1600
9³/₄ x 10 inches   19/9439

This may have been used to process
acorns, the staple food of the area.

28 Carved Jade Head
Olmec. Palenque, Mexico
1250-800 B.C.
Height: 2³/₄ inches   4/6274

An outstanding sculpture from one of
the earliest cultures in Mexico.
Collected about 1895 by Julius A.
Skilton.

29 Votive Hacha
Olmec. Veracruz, Mexico
1000 B.C.-250 A.D.
Height: 11¹/₂ inches   16/3400

Such large anthropomorphic stone
carvings are typical of the Olmec
culture. Collected by Leo Stein, presented by Thea Heye.

30 Carved Stone Effigy
Olmec. Alta Verapaz, Guatemala
1000-500 B.C.
Height: 9³/₄ inches   15/3560

With its head partly hollowed out, this
may have been an incense burner. An
example of the "baby-faced" type of
Olmec design. Collected by Samuel K.
Lothrop.

31 Standing Female Effigy
Tlatilco. Mexico, Mexico, 1000-700 B.C.
Height: 22 inches   23/4999

This large redware figurine has the
rounded quality of the art of the
Preclassic period in central Mexico.

32 Animal Effigy
Tlatilco. Mexico, Mexico, 1000-700 B.C.
7 x 10¹/₂ inches   23/6193

This painted *javelina* with rocker-
stamped decoration, the body painted
in red brown, is an example of an
early modeled clay effigy. Collected by
Miguel Covarrubias.

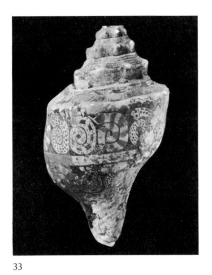

33

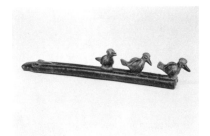

35

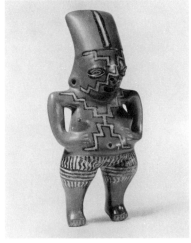

38

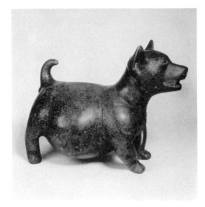

34

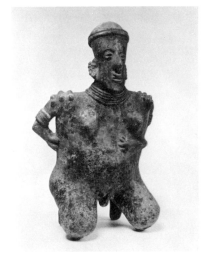

37

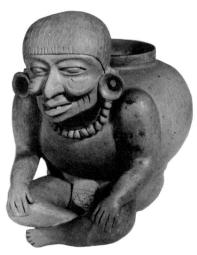

39

33 Painted Shell Trumpet
Chupícuaro. Guanajuato, Mexico
Circa 250 B.C.
Length: 9¹/₂ inches   24/2892

It is remarkable that the design of
serpents on a scroll pattern, painted
with fresco colors around the central
part of this conch shell, has survived.
Normally, all color is lost from old
objects of such a fragile nature.

34 Redware Dog Effigy
Los Ortices. Colima, Mexico
100 B.C.-250 A.D.
13 x 18 x 10 inches   23/8366

Larger than usual, this figure represents
a type of dog raised for food by the
early peoples of western Mexico. Such
effigies were often placed in graves to
assure the dead person of sustenance
in the next world. Presented by Dr. and
Mrs. Arthur M. Sackler.

35 Double Flute
Los Ortices. Colima, Mexico
100 B.C.-250 A.D.
Length: 19¹/₂ inches   24/7525

This 8-note blackware flute, decorated
with carefully crafted birds, is in
perfect condition. Presented by Mr.
and Mrs. Lee Goodman.

36 El Pensador Effigy   (frontispiece)
Buena Vista. Colima, Mexico
100 B.C.-250 A.D.
Height: 8¹/₂ inches   22/5100

Ceramics from Colima are noted for
their sculptural quality. This exquis-
itely modeled Tarascan redware figurine
was presented by John S. Williams.

37 Clay Birth Effigy
Mexpan. Nayarit, Mexico
100 B.C -350 A.D.
Height: 20 inches   24/7505

A large hollow ceramic figurine with
red and white decoration portraying a
woman in childbirth. The size is
unusual, and the subject is rare in pre-
Columbian art. Presented by Mr. and
Mrs. Francesco Pellizzi.

38 Standing Clay Figurine
Chupícuaro. Guanajuato, Mexico
100 B.C.-250 A.D.
6¹/₂ x 12 inches   24/7600

From the Preclassic period of western
Mexico. Presented by Dick Cavett.

39 Effigy
Teotihuacán. Toluca, Mexico, 250-650
Height: 12¹/₂ inches   16/6067

This seated representation of the deity
Huehuetéotl is modeled with extraordinary sensitivity.

31

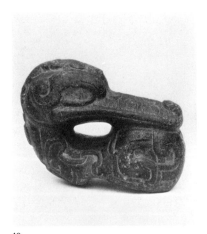

40

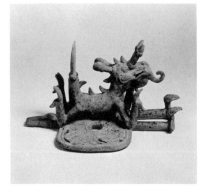

42

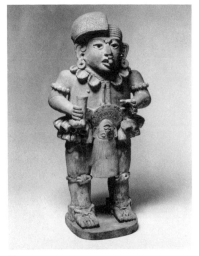

41

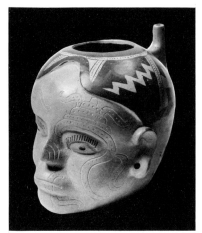

43

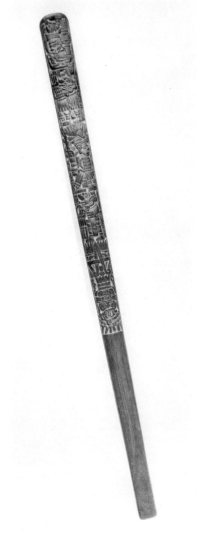

44

40 Stone Duck Head
Zacatecas, Mexico, 300-1200
Length: 6 inches   17/7375

The incised lines are typical of the El Tajín style.

41 Standing Clay Sculpture
Monte Albán. Mitla, Mexico 550-750
Height: 29 inches   19/5806

Apparently a Zapotec priest wearing a trophy head around his neck, with a belt of shells around his waist and a paw-shaped cup in one hand. Collected in 1845 by the French consul at Oaxaca, M. Martin.

42 Large Double Flute
Las Tuxtlas. Veracruz, Mexico, 900-1100
6 x 11½ inches   24/2715

The monster on this instrument is of a type found in East Coast Mexico. A clay pebble in each tube provided a sliding sound when the flute was blown.

43 Spouted Head Effigy Vessel
Huástec. Veracruz, Mexico, 900-1200
7 x 9 inches   24/3351

Both the intriguing modeling and the fine condition of this vessel are remarkable. Ceramics from this region are not common: they reflect a Mayoid influence. Presented by Mr. and Mrs. Donald C. Webster.

44 Carved Wooden Atlatl
Mixtec. Puebla, Mexico, 1300-1521
Length: 21½ inches   10/8724

Atlatls enhanced the power of the arm when one "threw" an arrow or short spear. An atlatl carved as carefully as this would have belonged to an important or wealthy person.

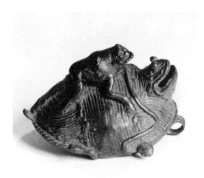

45

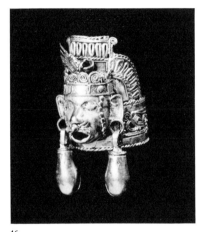

46

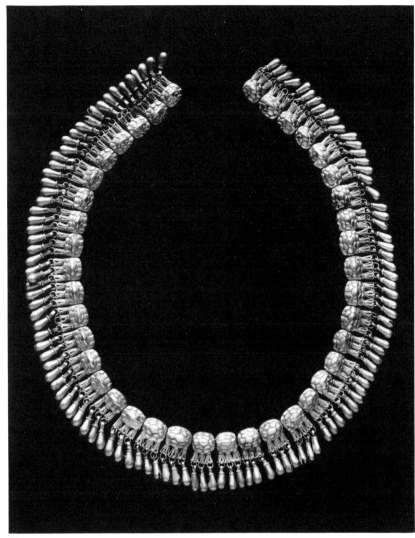

47

5 Cast Copper Bell
Los Ortices. Colima, Mexico
1250-1500
Height: 3¹/₂ inches   24/3191

This bell portrays one frog on top of
another. It has a solid copper clapper.

6 Cast Gold Ring
Mixtec. Oaxaca, Mexico, 1300-1521
⁷/₈ x 1³/₈ inches   20/6218

Made by the lost-wax process, this
shows, in delicate tracery, a death's
head, presumably a reference to the
Xipe Totec cult.

47 Gold Necklace
Mixtec. Sola de Vega, Mexico
1300-1521
Length: 14 inches   16/3451

Three tiny bells with gold clappers hang
from each of the forty turtle-shell-
shaped segments, demonstrating the
goldsmith's technical skill. Presented
by Thea Heye.

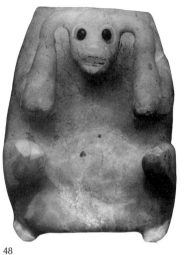

48

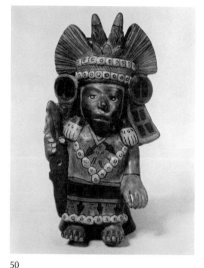

50

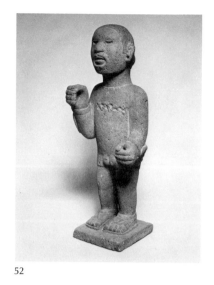

52

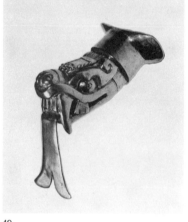

49

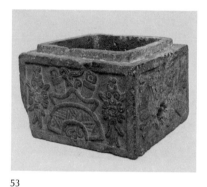

53

48 Alabaster Effigy Vessel

Mixtec. Isla de Sacrificios, Mexico
1300-1521
Height: 7⁷/₈ inches   16/3371

Carved in *tecali*, the form of calcite
frequently used in ancient Mexico, this
represents a seated monkey, with eyes
of inlaid obsidian discs. Excavated in
1827. Collected by Leo Stein, presented
by Thea Heye.

49 Cast Gold Labret

Mixtec. Oaxaca, Mexico, 1300-1521
2¹/₂ x 2¹/₂ inches   18/756

In the form of a serpent (or jaguar?)
with a separate, movable tongue, this
adornment was cast in the lost-wax
process. Wealthy persons wore such
objects in their lower lip. Weight,
70 grams.

50 Painted Clay Figurine

Mixteca-Puebla. Puebla, Mexico
1350-1520
Height: 13¹/₄ inches   23/6188

The figure, retaining much of its
original color, holds a flint weapon in
one hand. Presented by Dr. and Mrs.
Arthur M. Sackler.

51 Polychrome Vase

Cholula. Puebla, Mexico, 1350-1520
Height: 10 inches   16/3394

Such vessels impressed the Spaniards
as being superior to ceramics then
produced in Spain. Collected by Leo
Stein, presented by Thea Heye.

52 Statue of Xipe Totec

Tepepán. Mexico, Mexico, 1507
Height: 30¹/₂ inches   16/3621

Such figures, made of volcanic stone,
represented Xipe Totec, the Flayed
God, and were set up as standard
bearers outside Aztec temples. This
one has carved on its back the date
I Actl (1507), the year of the New Fire
ceremony.

53 Tepetlacalli

Aztec. Mexico, Mexico, 1440-1521
13 x 13 inches   1/6663

Containers of this form, carved of
volcanic stone, held blood and hearts
during sacrificial ceremonies. Collected
by Zelia Nuttall.

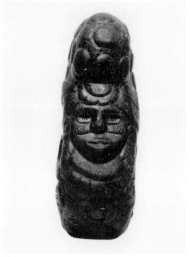

54

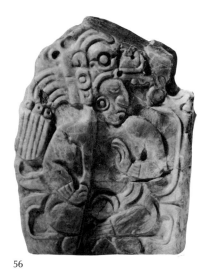

56

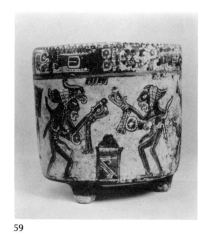

59

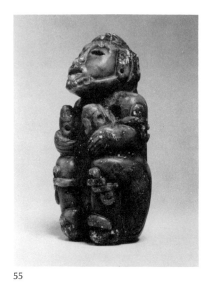

55

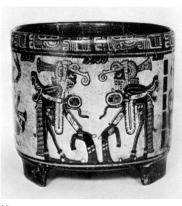

57

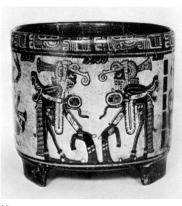

60

59 Polychrome Tripod Vase
Maya. Copán, Honduras, 550-950
Height: 8¹/₄ inches   24/4275

The painted designs represent two
priests with fans performing a ceremony
at an altar. Presented by Alice K. Bache.

54 Jadeite Quetzalcóatl Figurine
Aztec. Mexico, Mexico, 1440-1521
Height: 11¹/₄ inches   16/3467

The Plumed Serpent God of prehistoric
Mexican mythology is represented
with his elaborate feathered costume
effectively framing the central head
design.

55 Snake Priest Figurine
Maya? Chalchuapa, Santa Ana
El Salvador, 100 B.C.-250 A.D.
Height: 8¹/₂ inches   24/2082

Of green steatite, this figurine holds
serpents in each hand. His head is in
the jaws of a much larger reptile which
curves down his back. Two serpent
heads are on the headdress. Found
about 1900.

56 Jade Plaque
Monte Albán. Oaxaca, Mexico, 500-900
2¹/₄ x ¹/₄ x 3 inches   2/6671

This is a portrait of a Mayan dignitary
in the cross-legged seated position
typical of the style, wearing an elaborately feathered headdress.

57 Painted Stucco Head
Mayan. Uxmal, Mexico, 500-900
Height: 8¹/₂ inches   8/1972

This stucco sculpture is unusual for
having retained its original color. The
head once graced the now-destroyed
wall of a structure at Uxmal. Collected
in 1910 by Thomas Gann.

58 Carved Jade   (see page 15)

60 Polychrome Tripod Vase
Maya. Yuscarán, El Paraíso, Honduras
550-950
7⁷/₈ x 9¹/₄ inches   6/1259

Here the designs are of two priests in
elaborate costumes facing one another,
perhaps in a ritual. Collected by
Marco A. Soto, presented by Harmon
W. Hendricks.

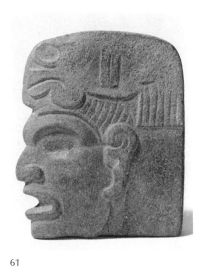

61

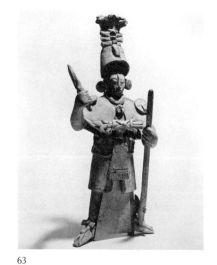

63

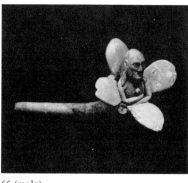

66 (male)

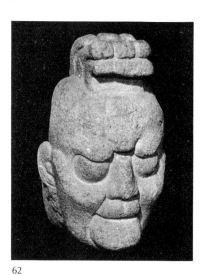

62

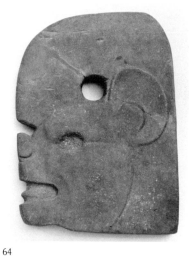

64

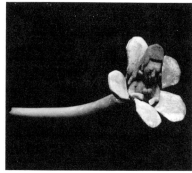

66 (female)

66 Pair of Clay Whistles
Maya. Jaina Island, Mexico, 550-900
Male: 4¹/₂ inches
Female: 5¹/₂ inches   24/451

These delicately modeled whistles, retaining some of their original paint, may have served as ear ornaments. Presented by Dr. and Mrs. Arthur M. Sackler.

61 Carved Stone Hacha
Maya. Santa Lucía Cotzumalhuapa
Guatemala, 550-950
7¹/₂ x 9¹/₂ inches   15/5708

Depicts a man wearing a zoömorphic headdress. Such objects were probably architectural ornaments. Presented by Harmon W. Hendricks.

62 Carved Stone Head
Maya. Quiriguá, Guatemala, 550-950
Height: 9¹/₂ inches   9/8199

This finely carved head bears similiarities to Japanese No art. It was once tenoned into the wall of Quiriguá. Collected by Marshall H. Saville in 1920, presented by James B. Ford.

63 Costumed Nobleman
Maya. Jaina Island, Mexico, 550-900
Height: 11¹/₂ inches   22/6348

This remarkably detailed ceramic figurine, possibly of a priest, shows the elaborate costume of the period. He holds a knife and a staff, and wears a conical hat. Presented by John S. Williams.

64 Carved Stone Hacha
Maya. Escuintla, Guatemala, 550-950
8 x 11¹/₂ inches   15/3561

Depicts the head of a bat, one of the major Mayan deities.

65 Standing Figurine   (see page 13)

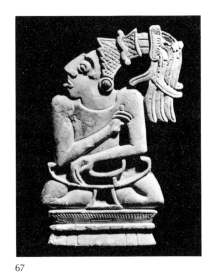

67

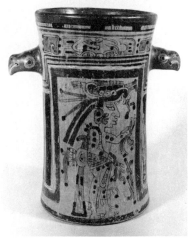

70

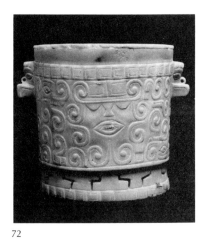

72

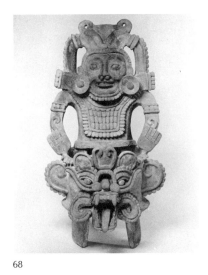

68

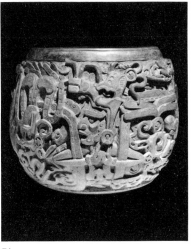

71

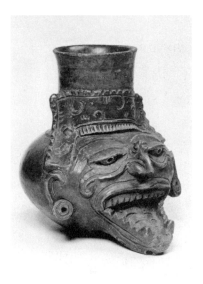

73

67 Shell Plaque
Maya. Palenque, Mexico, circa 900
Height: 2³/₄ inches   22/4955
A delicately carved profile of a Mayan noble seated on a low throne, once entirely inlaid with precious stones. All that now remains is the tiny pearl inset in the ear plug. Presented by Mr. and Mrs. Lou R. Crandall.

68 Clay Incense Burner
Maya. Alta Verapaz, Guatemala
900-1200
29 x 16 inches   23/6125
Modeled in the form of a Mayan deity or priest wearing a quilted garment, seated on a brazier edge. Presented by Stanley R. Grant.

69 Plumbate Effigy Vessel   (see page 14)

70 Polychrome Vase
Maya. Ulua Valley, Ulua, Honduras
700-900
Height: 9¹/₄ inches   22/4870
The design of this flamboyantly costumed Mayan noble is typical of the art style from the more southerly Maya region. This vessel has a pair of bird-head adornos on the sides, similar to the protruding heads on the better-known alabaster vases. Presented by John S. Williams.

71 Clay Bowl
Maya. San Augustín Acasaguastlán
Guatemala, 700-1000
7¹/₂ x 8 inches   20/7626
This elaborately modeled and carved container incorporates monkeys, serpents, and Mayan deities in a complex pattern. Presented by Harmon W. Hendricks.

72 Carved Alabaster Vase
Ulua Valley. Ulua, Honduras, 550-950
Height: 5⁷/₈ inches   6/1262
Commonly called marble vases, containers of this type seem to have originated in a very limited region, though they have been found widespread. Little is known of their iconography; they suggest a combination of Toltec and Tajín art styles. Collected by Marco A. Soto, presented by Harmon W. Hendricks.

73 Plumbate Vessel
Maya. San Salvador, El Salvador
950-1200
6¹/₄ x 7 inches   24/7225
This representation of the Fire God, one of the finest modeled heads of the type, comes from near the heart of the plumbate-producing region. Presented by Theodore T. Foley.

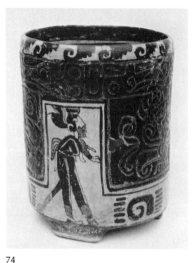

74

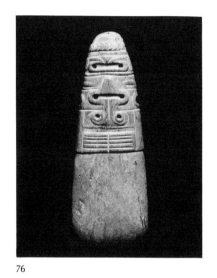

76

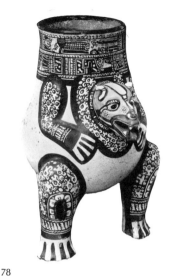

78

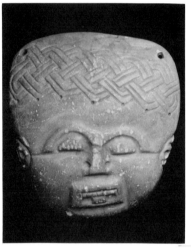

75

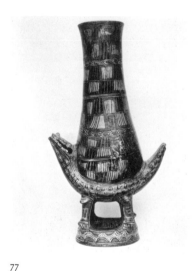

77

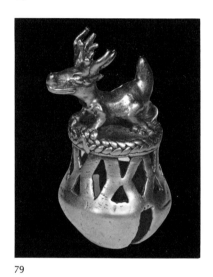

79

74 Polychrome Vase
Maya. San Salvador, El Salvador, 550-950
6¹/₂ x 8 inches   9/9572

This combination of incised and painted decoration forms an attractive design on a vessel typical of the region. Collected in 1919 by Marshall H. Saville, presented by James B. Ford.

75 Steatite Mask
Pipil. Morazán, El Salvador, 900-1200
6³/₄ x 7¹/₄ inches   13/601

Stone masks are uncommon south of Guatemala; this is one of two known from the Pipil area. The guilloche banding is frequently seen in Pipil art. Collected in 1925 by Samuel K. Lothrop.

76 Jade Ax God
Nicoya. Guanacaste, Costa Rica
300 B.C.-300 A.D.
Length: 7 inches   24/809

Formed from half of a jadeite celt, the design apparently represents a serpent head. The piece shows the string-sawed technique of separation on the back, and has been drilled, apparently so it could be worn as an ornament.

77 Polychrome Atlantean Vase
Filadelfía, Guanacaste, Costa Rica
750-1000
Height: 21 inches   19/4981

Gracefully formed, the vessel is supported by a crocodile on a ring base.

78 Jaguar Effigy Vessel
El General, Nicoya, Costa Rica, 800-1200
Height: 14 inches   19/4896

The smooth transition from animal head into the globular body that forms the container makes this a harmonious as well as a functional vessel. The legs have pebbles, making this a rattle vase. A remarkable amount of the original paint survives.

79 Cast Gold Bell
Cartago, Las Mercédes, Costa Rica
800-1525
Height: 3 inches   5/9849

Representing a tiny stag standing on the body of the bell, and fitted with a solid gold clapper, this was probably worn or carried as an ornament. Weight, 77 grams.

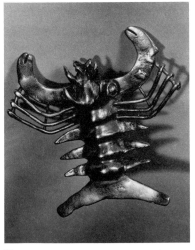

80

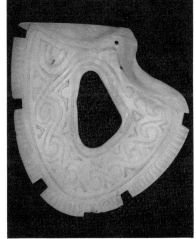

82

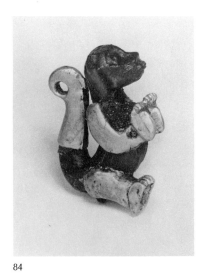

84

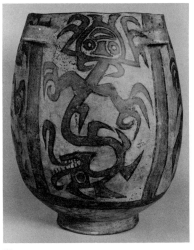

83

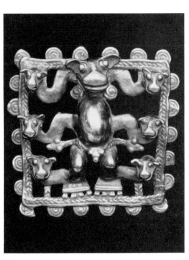

86

80 Gold Pendant
Cartago, Las Mercédes, Costa Rica
800-1525
3¹/₂ x 3¹/₄ inches   5/9847

Cast by the lost-wax process, this well-balanced and beautifully detailed design represents a crayfish. Weight, 79 grams.

81 Sheet Gold Helmet
Parita. Azuero Peninsula, Panama
1000-1500
9 x 3¹/₂ x 8¹/₄ inches   23/2339

Carefully hammered out and incised with scroll designs, this is the type of helmet seen on many stone carvings from this region. The advanced stage of goldsmithing in the Isthmus provided the main cause for the Spanish invasion of the early sixteenth century. The size of this object suggests that it was worn with a textile bandeau sewn to the holes around the rim.

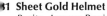

81

82 Incised Shell Pendant
Venado Beach. Canal Zone, Panama
500-750
Length: 5 inches   22/5271

The design is of a type seen most frequently on Coclé pottery. The pendant was probably worn on the breast as a gorget.

83 Clay Urn
Chiriquí. Río Tabasará, Panama
800-1200
14 x 17 inches   22/9301

Large vessels of this shape are not common in the region, and this urn is in unusually fine condition. The double-headed reptile design is often seen in less angular form. Presented by Peter J. Potoma, Jr.

84 Copal Monkey
Parita. Azuero Peninsula, Panama
1250-1500
Height: 2³/₄ inches   23/2352

The figure has been fitted with thin sheet-gold legs, tail, and jaw. While the gold overlay from such objects is often found, the resinous copal has usually disappeared. Presented by Alex Stephenson.

85 Polychrome Frutera   (see page 20)

86 Gold Buckle
Chiriquí. Bugaba, Panama, 800-1525
3 x 3 inches   8263

Cast by the lost-wax process. Six jaguar heads surround the large jaguar; there is a gold clapper in his belly. Collected in 1906 by Frank D. Utley. Weight, 156 grams.

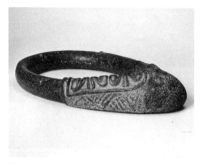

87

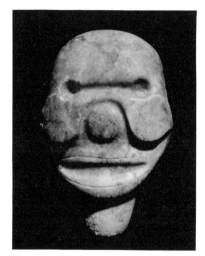

89

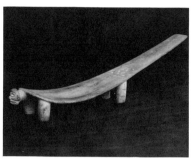

91

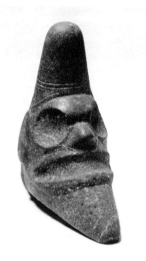

88

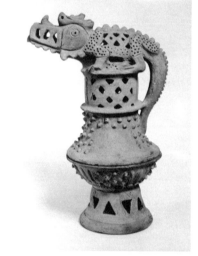

90

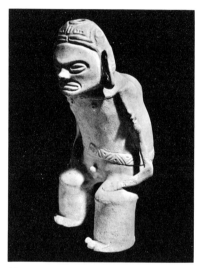

92

87 Carved Stone Collar
Taíno. Arecibo, Puerto Rico, 1000-1500
11 x 18 inches   1/6662

Believed to have served a function
similar to that of the carved stone yokes
found throughout Middle America,
such collars occur in several distinct
styles. Their design is also seen in
pottery and wood carvings from the
Caribbean area.

88 Carved Tri-Point Stone
Taíno. Puerto Rico, 1000-1500
7¹/₂ x 7 inches   19/917

Such finely worked objects are thought
to have served as ceremonial objects.
Commonly called a *zemi* (spirit) they
occur in various combinations of
designs. Collected by Jesse Walter
Fewkes.

89 Carved Stone Death Head
Taíno. Arecibo, Puerto Rico, 1000-1500
4¹/₂ x 7 inches   23/6096

The practice of taking trophy heads
may have been familiar to the Taíno
people. Many such carvings have been
found. Collected by Salvador López
de Azua.

90 Ceramic Incense Burner
Ometepe Island. Lake Nicaragua
Rivas, Nicaragua, 1000-1500
Height: 18 inches   23/4043

Such burners are found in the southern
Nicaragua-Costa Rica region. They
are fragile, and complete ones are rare.

91 Wooden Seat
Taíno. Turks Island, Bahamas, 1000-1500
Length: 33¹/₂ inches   5/9385

The *duho,* a form of backrest or
"chief's seat," was used throughout the
West Indies. This type of furniture had
its origins in northern South America.
Collected by Lady Edith Blake.

92 Hunchback Effigy
Taíno. Andrés, Dominican Republic
1000-1500
Height: 16 inches   5/3753

Worked in very thin-walled buff clay.
Found by Theodoor deBooy in 1916, set
up on an altar in a cave.

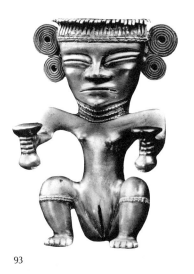

93

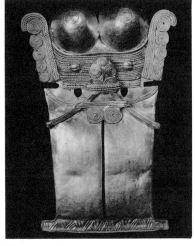

95

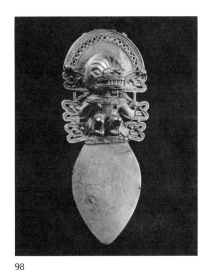

98

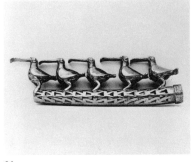

96

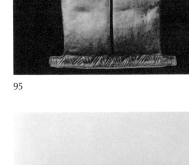

94

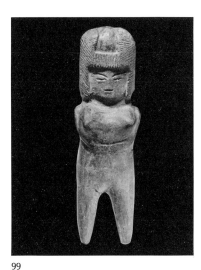

99

93 Gold Figurine
Quimbaya. Medellín, Colombia
750-1500
Height: 1⁷/₈ inches   23/6499

A hollow cast effigy of a seated female with an elaborate headdress, holding small buckskin bags of gold dust in her hands. Presented by Dr. and Mrs. Arthur M. Sackler. Weight, 55.5 grams.

94 Gold Pendant
Sinú. Rio Sinú, Colombia, 700-1500
6¹/₂ x 10¹/₄ inches   5/2841

This sheet-gold breast ornament is unique in that it has a row of bird cut-outs across the face. It was found in a tomb before 1909 by F. A. Scharberg. Presented by Thea Heye. Weight, 672 grams.

95 Gold Pendant
Sinú. Rio Sinú, Colombia, 700-1500
6 x 9 inches   5/2842

This magnificent hammered object represents a highly stylized creature holding batons in its hands. Found in a tomb before 1909 by F. A. Scharberg. Presented by Thea Heye. Weight, 550 grams.

96 Cast Gold Staff Head
Sinú. Rio Nechí, Colombia, 1000-1500
2¹/₄ x 8 inches   10/507

This beautifully proportioned finial demonstrates the ability of the ancient Sinú artists to cast gold in large pieces. Excavated along the Nechí River in 1898 by A. F. Dovale. Presented by Harmon W. Hendricks. Weight, 508 grams.

97 Jaguar Effigy Vessel   (see page 12)

98 Cast Gold Spatula
Tairona. Santa Marta, Colombia
1250-1500
Length: 4³/₈ inches   24/7980

Perhaps used by a wealthy individual in taking coca. Presented by Alice K. Bache. Weight, 35.5 grams.

99 Clay Figurine
Valdivia. Ecuador, circa 3000 B.C.
Height: 3¹/₄ inches   24/8400

This female figure from near the mouth of the Guayas River represents the earliest New World culture from which ceramics have yet been found. Presented by Alice K. Bache.

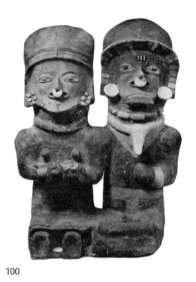

100

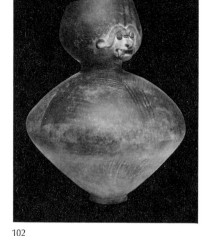

102

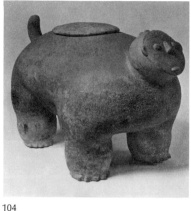

104

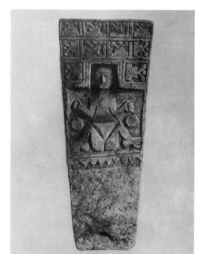

101

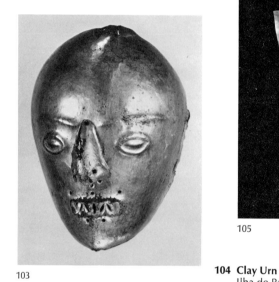

103

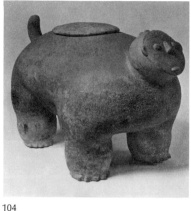

105

100 Seated Family Group
Bahía. Manabí, Ecuador
500 B.C.-500 A.D.
17 x 22 inches   23/7000

A man, his wife, and their child—a common theme in prehistoric ceramics. The large size and remaining color make this an unusual work. Presented by Dr. and Mrs. Arthur M. Sackler.

101 Carved Stone Stela
Manteño. Cerro Jaboncillo, Ecuador
800-1400
18 x 40 inches   1/4473

This bas-relief represents a woman with repeat geometric designs framing her head. Collected in 1907 by Marshall H. Saville.

102 Blackware Burial Urn
Manteño. Enseñada, Ecuador, 800-1400
Height: 21 inches   1/4947

The modeled face of a *tigre* appears on the upper portion, matte-finished linear decorations on the lower part. Collected by Marshall H. Saville.

103 Gold Mask
Manteño. Manabí, Ecuador, 800-1400
5¹/₂ x 7¹/₂ inches   24/7533

Hammered out of sheet copper and heavily plated with gold, the nose is detachable. Presented by Dick Cavett.

104 Clay Urn
Ilha de Pará, Amazonas, Brazil
1000-1250
14 x 25¹/₂ inches   18/1956

This animal-shaped urn was used to hold bones, following an initial interment, in a custom called secondary burial. Collected by William C. Farabee in 1913.

105 Gold Crown
Sigsig. Azuay, Ecuador, 1000-1500
7¹/₂ x 14 inches   1/2062

Headbands of this type were worn with textile bands into which the gold plumes were thrust. This is part of the famed Treasure of Sigsig, found in 1889. Presented by Marie A. Heye.

106 Gold Crown   (see page 17)

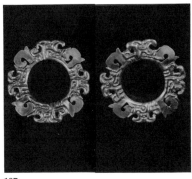

107

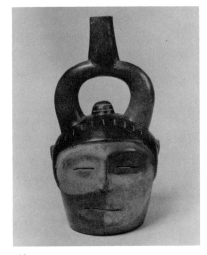

109

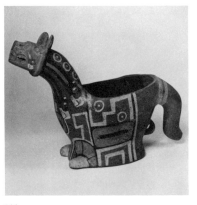

111

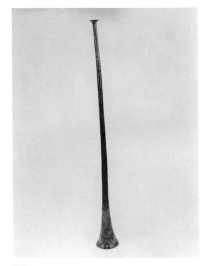

108

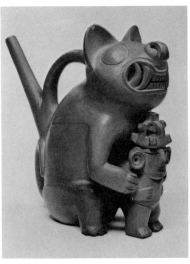

110

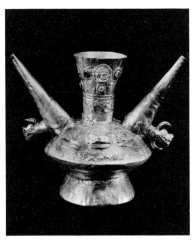

113

07 Gold Ear Spools
Coastal Chavín. Chongoyape, Peru
900-500 B.C.
Diameter: 5 inches   16/1972F

Such cut-out discs with repoussé
decoration were worn by wealthy
Peruvian nobles. Found with number
106.

08 Ceramic Trumpet
Paracas. Juan Pablo, Ica Valley, Peru
500-250 B.C.
Length: 54 inches   24/1890

A practical instrument, delicately
crafted, and an unusual survivor in view
of its large size.

109 Painted Stirrup-Spout Vessel
Tembladera. Cajamarca, Peru
250 B.C.-250 A.D.
Length: 12¹/₂ inches   24/7645

This head vessel shows the high quality
of early Chavín ceramics. Presented
by Dick Cavett.

110 Orange Ware Effigy Vessel
Gallinazo. Viru, Peru
Circa 500-100 B.C.
7³/₄ x 8¹/₂ inches   24/7550

One of the more famous specimens of
its type, this portrays the "alter ego"
design frequently found in American
Indian art. Collected by James A. Ford,
presented by Dr. and Mrs. Frederick
J. Dockstader.

111 Painted Clay Puma
Tiahuanaco. La Paz, Bolivia, 750-1000
11¹/₂ x 16 inches   23/7095

This gracefully proportioned vessel
may have been used as an incense
burner. The tail is restored. Presented
by Dr. and Mrs. Arthur M. Sackler.

112 Polychrome Urn   (see page 9)

113 Spouted Vessel
Chimú. Lambayeque, Peru, 1350-1470
7¹/₂ x 9 inches   24/7975

This elaborate vessel in sheet gold is of
a type frequently seen in clay; silver
examples are also known. It was a
favorite design of early Chimú artists.
Presented by Alice K. Bache.

43

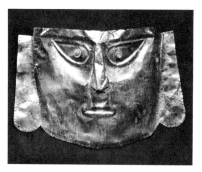

114

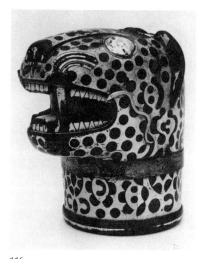

116

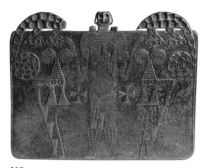

118

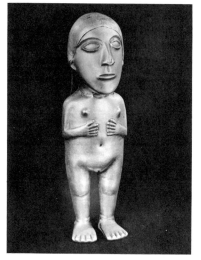

115

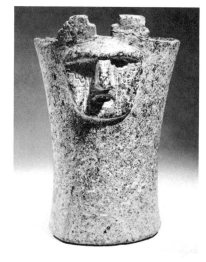

117

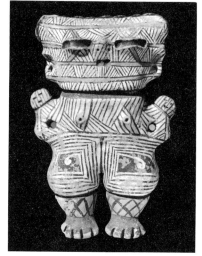

119

114 Gold Mask
Chimú. Lambayeque, Peru, 1350-1476
11 x 18 inches   18/4291

Of hammered sheet gold with small
turquoise-bead eyes. This type of mask
was attached to the mummy bundles
of wealthy Peruvians.

115 Gold Effigy
Inca. Coastal Peru, circa 1500
Height: 9¹/₂ inches   5/4120

This hollow female figurine is remarkable both for its graceful modeling and
large size. Obtained in Panama in
1916. Weight, 511 grams.

116 Painted Wooden Kero
Inca. Cuzco, Peru, 1550-1600
Height: 9 inches   10/5860

Typical of the art of the Inca craftsman
at the time of the Spanish Conquest.
The ocelot's eyes, collar, and overlaid
serpent whiskers are of silver. Collected
by A. Hyatt Verrill.

117 Steatite Kero
Condorhuasi. Argentina, 250-500
Height: 9¹/₄ inches   24/2898

With a puma head carved on one side,
this vessel shows Inca influence in the
southern part of the continent.
Presented by Dick Cavett.

118 Cast Bronze Plaque
Atacameño. Salta, Argentina, 1250-1500
6 x 7³/₄ inches   20/8192

Such finely worked plaques are found
in the Calchaquí region. This example
was collected before 1854 by Captain
Theodore Canot.

119 Madonna Effigy
El Tocuyo. Lara, Venezuela, 500-1500
Height: 8¹/₂ inches   4/8740

A modeled and painted figurine, in the
Betijoque style, of a woman with her
two babies, the latter formed by
extensions of her arms. Collected by
C. F. Witzke before 1900.

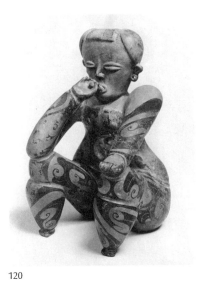

120

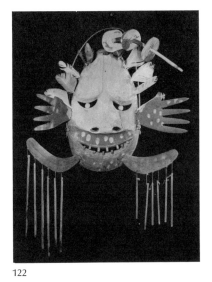

122

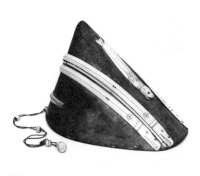

124

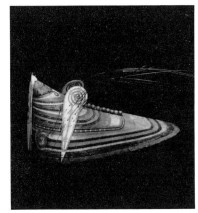

125

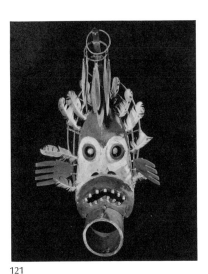

121

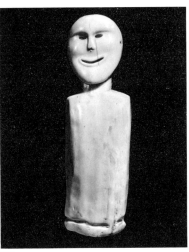

123

124 Hunter's Hat

Eskimo. Yukon River, Alaska, circa 1850
Length: 13½ inches   10/6921

Worked from thin sheets of wood and
decorated with strips of walrus ivory,
this has linear designs similar to those
of prehistoric Bering Sea art. The form
is similar to that of Aleut hats.

125 Painted Hunting Hat

Aleut. Aleutian Islands, Alaska
Circa 1825
Length: 16 inches   14/4869

Decorated with painted designs, trade
beads, ivory, and sea lion whiskers,
such hats were worn by men of high
status for hunting sea otters. The
designs have symbolic significance, and
the hats were believed to attract the
animals. Presented by Thea Heye.

120 El Fumador Effigy

Trujillo. Venezuela, 500-1500
Height: 10¾ inches   11/2852

A hollow ceramic figurine of a seated
woman smoking a cigar. The decorations consist of black curvilinear
designs in the Santa Ana style. Presented
by E. J. Sadler.

121 Wooden Dance Mask

Kuskwogmiut Eskimo. Kuskokwim River
Alaska, 1875-1890
Height: 30 inches   9/3430

This represents Negakfok, the Cold
Weather Being, who likes winter and
storms, and who appeared to a shaman
and gave him supernatural powers.
He looks sad because he must leave the
people at the approach of spring.
Collected by A. H. Twitchell about
1885.

122 Wooden Dance Mask

Kuskwogmiut Eskimo. Kuskokwim River
Alaska, 1875-1890
Height: 20 inches   9/3432

Representing the spirit Walaunuk,
meaning "Bubbles as they rise up
through the water." Such masks are
frequently destroyed after their use
during the ceremonial season. Collected
by A. H. Twitchell about 1885.

123 Shaman's Doll

Eskimo. Point Barrow, Alaska, 1850-1875
Height: 9½ inches   7/7096

This sleek carving of walrus ivory has
inlaid copper eyes; it was once dressed.
Such figurines are used by shamans
in ceremonies.

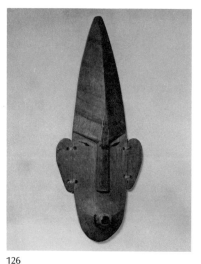

126

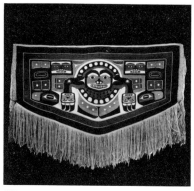

128

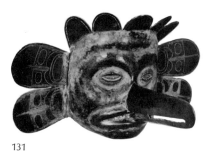

131

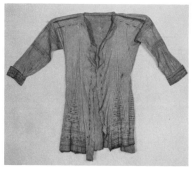

127

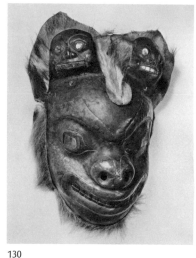

130

133

126 Wooden Mask

Ingalik. Anvik, Alaska, circa 1900
Height: 22½ inches   5/8667

Demonstrating the influence of Eskimo design upon neighboring Athapascan Indian peoples, this mask is used in the Gi-yema feast and represents one of the Up-river People. They are regarded as unsophisticated by their Down-river relatives. Collected by G. T. Emmons.

127 Painted Coat

Naskapi. Labrador, Canada, circa 1850
8 x 10 feet   2/9177

This semitailored reindeer-hide garment shows European influence. The symbolic painted designs assisted the hunter.

128 Ceremonial Robe

Tlingit. Chilkat, Alaska, circa 1900
5 x 6 feet   14/7330

The interweaving of mountain-sheep wool and cedar-bark fiber is a distinctive technique common to the Northwest Coast area. The animal designs more commonly seen in such robes give way here to a portrayal of the octopus. Collected by G. T. Emmons.

129 Canoe-Prow Effigy   (see page 23)

130 Copper Mask

Tlingit. Sitka, Alaska, circa 1875
9 x 16 inches   24/3149

The hammered and incised design represents the Brown Bear, a spiritual or mythological being. The trimmings are of bear fur and abalone shell; the teeth are of mountain-goat horn. Presented by Morton D. May.

131 Copper Mosquito Mask

Tlingit. Klukwan, Alaska, 1825-1850
8½ x 14 inches   6981

Decorated with abalone-shell inlays. The mosquito was one of several comic characters who performed in skits. Collected by B. A. Whalen.

132 Otter Woman Mask   (see page 11)

133 Shaman's Charm

Tlingit. Sitka, Alaska, 1825-1850
Length: 5 inches   9/7948

Carved from antler, this represents a spirit canoe in the shape of a sea lion, carrying the spirits of seven people drowned when the craft was seized by an octopus. Such charms were worn by the shaman to give him supernatural power. Collected by G. T. Emmons.

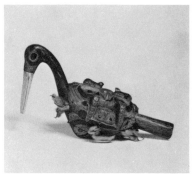

134

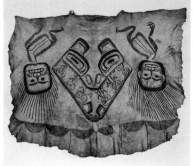

136

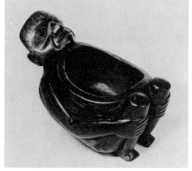

139

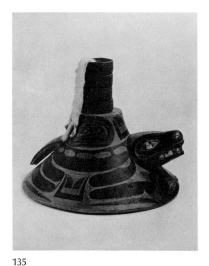

135

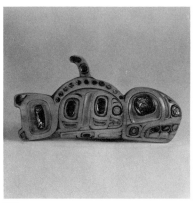

138

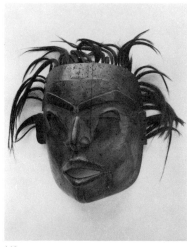

140

4 Chief's Rattle
Tlingit. Stikine, Etolin Island, Alaska
1850-1875
Length: 12 inches   23/5603

Carved from cedar in the form of a
crane with a bone beak. The body is
decorated with ermine strips, and
designs of octopus, killer whales, a
hawk, and a sea monster. Collected by
Judge Nathan Bijur from the family of
Chief Shaikes.

5 Wooden Crest Helmet
Tlingit. Sitka, Alaska, circa 1875
14½ x 20 inches   24/3378

Of cedar, the carving is decorated with
inlaid abalone shell and strips of
copper; the design represents the sea
lion. The four basketry cylinders at
the top denote the number of times its
owner had given a potlatch. Presented
by Mr. and Mrs. John DeMénil.

136 Shaman's Painted Robe
Tlingit. Stikine, Wrangell Island, Alaska
1850-1875
47 x 60 inches   1/2492

Of caribou hide, the painted bear-head
design with spirit *yeks* as teeth gives
the wearer added supernatural power.
Collected by G. T. Emmons.

137 Cedar Wood Rattle   (see page 18)

138 Ivory Shaman's Charm
Kitksan. Kitwanga, British Columbia
Circa 1850
Length: 6½ inches   9/7954

Carved and inlaid with abalone shell
to represent a killer whale, this was
fastened to the shaman's clothing and
used as a fetish. Collected by G. T.
Emmons.

139 Wooden Feast Dish
Tsimshian. Metlakatla, British Columbia
Circa 1875
4 x 8 inches   9/7881

Carved to represent a human figure,
dishes of this type were used at feasts
for holding the olachen oil in which
dried fish was dipped. Collected by
G. T. Emmons.

140 Classic Wooden Mask
Tsimshian. Skeena River
British Columbia, circa 1800
7 x 9½ inches   3/4678

Painted and decorated with human
hair, this is possibly a portrait. Such
realism is seen more frequently among
Tsimshian sculpture than in that of
most of the other Northwest Coast
tribes.

47

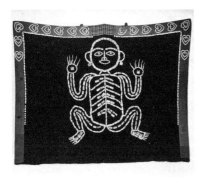

141

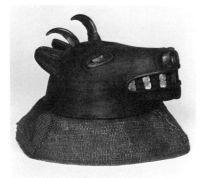

143

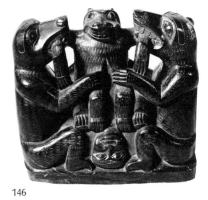

146

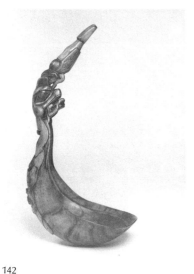

142

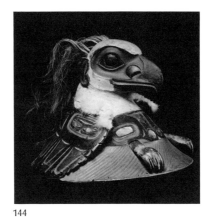

144

147

141 Button Blanket

Tlingit. Sitka, Alaska, circa 1880
56 x 73 inches   12/2564

Blue trade cloth, trimmed with red
stroud material. The pearl button and
dentalium-shell decoration represents a
human figure, probably the owner.
The rich abalone-shell ornamentation
added to the blanket's importance.
These were worn on ceremonial occasions by wealthy persons. Collected
by G. T. Emmons.

142 Horn Ladle

Haida. Queen Charlotte Islands
British Columbia, circa 1875
9 x 17 inches   9/8065

Made from the horn of the mountain
sheep, such ladles were used for serving
olachen oil. The designs represent
family crest figures, including bears, a
frog, and an owl. Collected by
G. T. Emmons.

143 Mountain Goat Helmet

Haida. Prince of Wales Island, Alaska
Circa 1825
10 x 15¹/₂ inches   21/439

The horns of this cedar wood helmet
are made from grizzly bear claws; the
inlay is abalone shell. The helmet is
sewn to a basketry base woven of cedar
bark. Presented by The Viking Fund,
Inc.

144 Wooden Crest Helmet

Haida. Prince of Wales Island, Alaska
Circa 1875
Height: 9¹/₂ inches   14/9081

Carved of cedar and painted to represent the eagle, this helmet is decorated
with abalone-shell inlay and human
hair. Though such helmets were once
used in warfare, they came to have
a major use as family crests at ceremonial occasions. Collected by G. T.
Emmons.

145 Carved Figurine   (see page 19)

146 Argillite Sculpture

Haida. Skidegate, Queen Charlotte
Islands, British Columbia, 1875-1900
7 x 7 inches   19/3521

Made of a stone—commonly called
slate—that is found only on the Queen
Charlotte Islands. This group represents
an episode in the legend of the Bear
Mother, in which the berry picker gives
birth to her bear child, assisted by
two grizzly bears. Interestingly, it
represents birth by Caesarian section.
Reputedly carved by Charles Edensaw.
Collected by William M. Fitzhugh.

147 Painted Wooden Rattle

Haida. Queen Charlotte Islands
British Columbia, circa 1850
Length: 12¹/₂ inches   1/8027

Such rattles were used by shamans. The
design shows a row of spirits surmount-
ing the central head of the beaver.
Collected by Reverend Thomas Crosby.

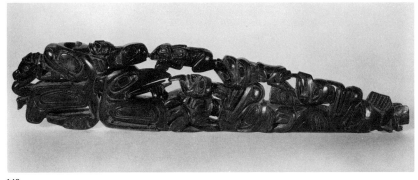

148

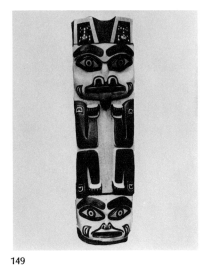

149

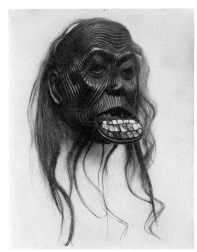

150

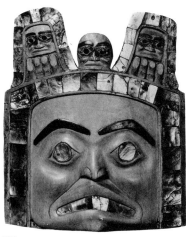

151

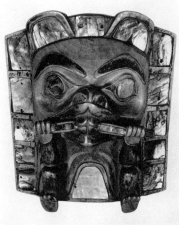

152

8 Argillite Pipe
Haida. Queen Charlotte Islands
British Columbia, circa 1832
Length: 13½ inches   1/9272

Such objects were carved in response
to demand from sailors and others. This
early example of an art that began
around 1800 was collected by Governor
William Clark, and given by him to
George Catlin, the artist, sometime
before 1832. Thomas Donaldson
Collection.

9 Wooden House Post
Haida. Cordova Bay, Alaska, circa 1850
4 x 11½ feet   15/9199

The design represents the Sea Bear,
and has a frog carved on each ear. This
was presented as a gesture of respect
to Chief Frog Ears of Sukkwan by the
inhabitants of a neighboring village.

150 Mask of an Old Woman
Niska. Upper Nass River
British Columbia, 1825-1850
7 x 9½ inches   9/8044

This portrait mask of a wealthy woman,
as evidenced by her elaborate labret
inlaid with abalone shell, represents a
tradition of portrait sculpture among
the Northwest Coast tribes. Collected
by G. T. Emmons.

151 Frontlet Headdress
Niska. Nass River, British Columbia
Circa 1875
6 x 7 inches   1/4294

Carved of cedar and inlaid with
abalone shell. The face may represent
the owner himself. Collected by G. T.
Emmons.

152 Frontlet Headdress
Niska. Nass River, British Columbia
Circa 1875
Height: 7½ inches   1/4295

Cedar wood inlaid with abalone shell.
The design represents the beaver.
Headdresses of this style were worn on
important occasions to indicate the
family or status of the wearer. Collected
by G. T. Emmons.

49

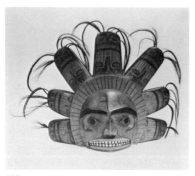

153

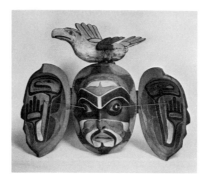

155

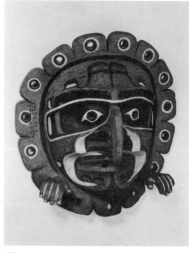

158

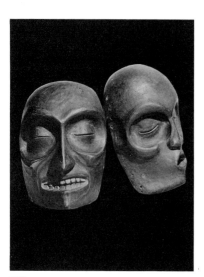

154

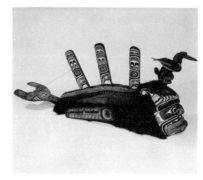

156

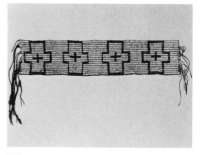

160

153 Carved Wooden Headdress
Niska. Nass River, British Columbia
Circa 1875
Height: 10¹/₂ inches   18/5783

Painted to represent the sun. Decorated
with human hair. Collected by George
G. Heye.

154 Dual Masks
Niska. Aiyansh, British Columbia
1850-1875
Height: 10 inches   1/4238

One depicts a cannibal spirit who lives
in the mountains, whistling to attract
the passer-by, the other represents his
victim. Collected by G. T. Emmons.

155 Movable Mask
Kwakiutl. Cape Mudge
British Columbia, 1850-1900
Height: 21¹/₂ inches   19/8963

Such masks were worn by shamans in
theatrical performances. Strings were
pulled to open the covering mask,
revealing the inner carving, often
portraying the spirit of the outer char-
acter, reflecting the dual quality of
many of the Northwest Coast mythological beings. Collected by George
G. Heye.

156 Mechanical Headdress
Kwakiutl. Cape Mudge
British Columbia, 1875-1900
30 x 66 inches   10/254

Representing a sea monster—perhaps
the Sea Bear—this has a bird atop a
human head. When the strings are
pulled, the dorsal and ventral fins
move, and the tail waves to move the
monster through the water. Worn on
the shoulders of the dancer, this is
supposed to start the salmon run in the
spring, frightening the fish toward
shore. Collected by George G. Heye.

157 Mechanical Headdress   (see page 21)

158 Octopus Spirit Mask
Kwakiutl. Cape Mudge
British Columbia, 1875-1900
20 x 22 inches   11/5216

The subject is indicated by the suckers,
hooked beak, and prominent eyes. A
fine example of symbolism in Northwest Coast art. Collected by George G.
Heye.

159 Wooden House Front   (see page 22)

160 Wampum Belt
Lenni Lenape (Delaware). Pennsylvania
1683
5¹/₄ x 24¹/₂ inches   5/3150

Wampum served as a gift, also as a
binding symbol of an agreement. This
belt was given to William Penn by
the Lenni Lenape in 1683 at the Treaty
of Shakamaxon, one of a number of
treaties by which the Quakers acquired
the land which later became the state
of Pennsylvania. The crosses symbolize
the land ceded. Presented by Harmon
W. Hendricks.

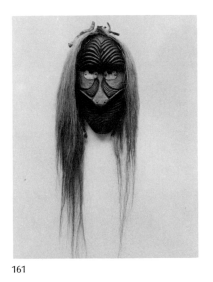

161

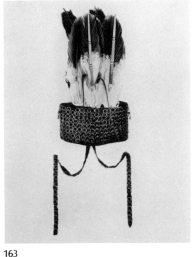

163

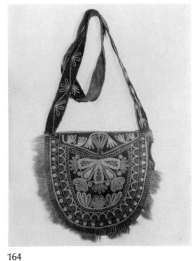

164

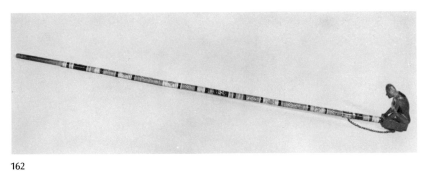

162

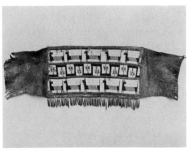

165

1 False Face Mask
Mohawk. Canada, circa 1775
Height: 12 inches   6/1104

One of the earliest-known dated False Face Society masks, this was taken to Canada by Joseph Brant at the time of the American Revolution. The Iroquois used such masks in healing ceremonies. Collected by Joseph Keppler, presented by Harriet M. Converse.

2 Pipe and Bowl
Mohawk. New York. Hallmark: 1789
Length: 33 inches   18/6071

The slate bowl is carved in the form of a seated figure; the wooden stem is covered with a porcupine-quill decoration. A silver band attached to the two parts bears the hallmark of Hester Bateman, a London silversmith. This was presented to Joseph Brant, the Mohawk leader, by Caleb Bingham.

163 Stand-Up Bonnet
Great Lakes. circa 1793
Length: 15 inches   24/2000

Decorated with eagle feathers, satin-wrapped birchbark headband, trade silver brooches, and porcelain trade beads, this is one of the earliest examples of the feather headdress of the Great Lakes area. It differs from the Plains bonnet in that it does not spread out from the base. Collected by Lieutenant Andrew Foster.

164 Moosehair Pouch
Huron. Canada, 1775-1800
8¹/₂ x 9 inches   11/5716

Made of dyed moosehair sewn onto a black-dyed deerskin base, with a fringe of red-dyed deer hair. The designs are those learned by young Indian girls in French convents.

165 Quillwork Panel
Lenni Lenape (Delaware). Pennsylvania
Circa 1800
Length: 14³/₄ inches   19/3264

Intended to be attached to the head of a baby carrier, this buckskin band is decorated with metal jinglers and a porcupine-quilled design in the Under-water Panther motif. This was made just before beads became plentiful. Collected by William M. Fitzhugh.

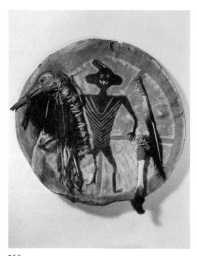

166

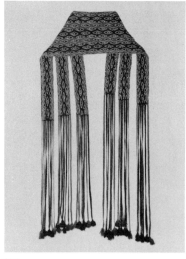

167

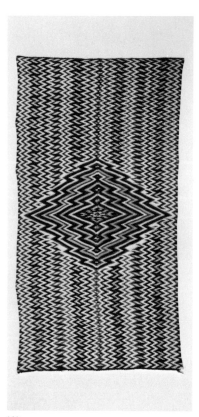

168

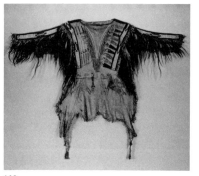

169

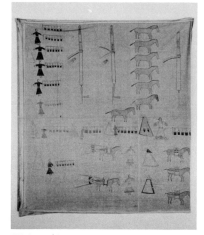

170 (panel I)

166 Painted Shield
Crow. Montana, 1800-1834
Diameter: 24 inches   11/7680

This belonged to Chief Arapoosh at the time of the Lewis and Clark Expedition. It was used for divining by rolling it along the ground. Success was assured if it stopped face up. If it fell with the design to the ground, the project in question would be abandoned. The design is of the Moon, which came to the owner in human form during a vision. Collected by William Wildschut.

167 Finger-Weave Sash
Lower Creek. Coweta, Georgia
Circa 1825
10 x 116 inches   24/2402

Woven for Chief William MacIntosh, the famous Creek leader, by his daughter. It is remarkable for its size. Presented by Rudolf G. Wunderlich.

168 Woolen Serape
Saltillo. Coahuila, Mexico, 1836
49 x 49 inches   24/3675

This is a fine example of the Saltillo weavings of central Mexico. It is notable for having belonged to General Antonio López y Santa Ana, who gave it to Sam Houston following the latter's victory at San Jacinto in 1836. The opportunity to date such specimens is rare. Presented by Mrs. Russell W. Todd.

169 Painted Buckskin Shirt
Cheyenne. Fort Laramie, Wyoming
1850
Length (open): 55 inches   8/8034

Decorated with quillwork, beading, scalp locks, and representations of men on horseback and a visionary experience of the owner. Such shirts were thought to protect the wearer in battle. Collected in 1850 by Thomas S. Twiss, Indian Agent at Fort Laramie. Presented by Harmon W. Hendricks.

170 Painted Tipi Liner
Sioux. South Dakota, 1877
62 x 198 inches   20/5176

Late in the nineteenth century government-issue muslin was frequently used for liners to ventilate the tipi; these were decorated with the owner's exploits. This example, painted by Strike-the-Kettle, depicts a Dog Feast, held by the Sioux to celebrate their victory over Custer.

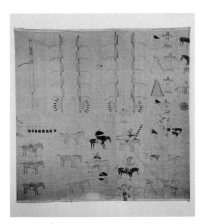

170 (panel II)

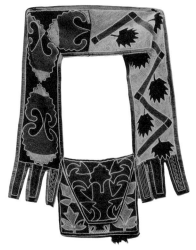

171

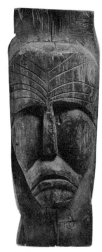

173 (front view)

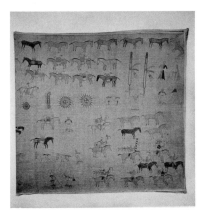

170 (panel III)

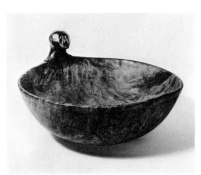

172

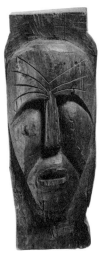

173 (back view)

171 Beaded Shoulder Pouch
Shawnee. Oklahoma, circa 1825
Length: 29 inches
Pouch: 8 x 8 inches   10/3133

Patterned after early bullet pouches, or perhaps the side pockets of Colonial military uniforms, such beautifully worked pouches were important parts of Indian dress in the 18th and 19th centuries. The shoulder strap was normally designed in two quite different halves, as in this example. Collected by Dr. W. C. Barnard.

172 Ceremonial Bowl
Sauk. Oklahoma, circa 1850
Diameter: 17 inches   2/6544

The Eastern Woodlands people favored ceremonial bowls carved from burls. The effigies depicted here were spirits related to the Midéwewin rites. Collected by M. R. Harrington.

173 Carved Center Post
Lenni Lenape (Delaware)
Dewey, Oklahoma, circa 1880
Length: 26½ inches   16/4844

One of the posts that supported the roof of the ceremonial Long House at Copan. It is one of the few remnants of ancient culture which was taken west with the Delaware Removal. The design represents the Meesing, a Delaware deity.

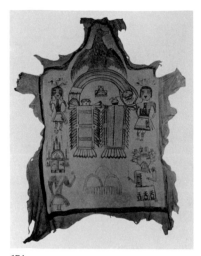

174

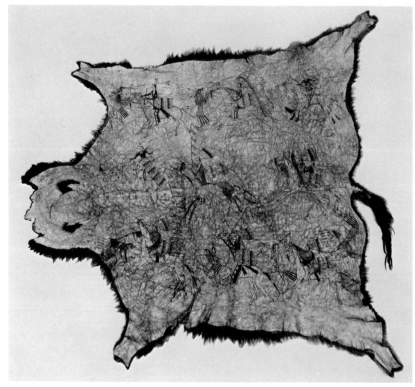

176

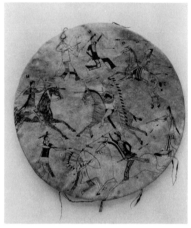

175

176 War Scene on Buffalo Hide

Oglala Sioux. Pine Ridge, South Dakota
1875-1880
64 x 82 inches   522

Designs of this type were always painted
by men (women painted geometric
motifs). Here we see the owner in the
center, with several companions, fight-
ing the Crow. Collected in 1880 from
Young Man Afraid of His Horses
(Tasunka-kokipapi), a Dakota leader.

174 Painted Elkskin

Hopi Pueblo. Oraibi, Arizona, circa 1900
Length: 75 inches   9/7656

The art of painting on hide is less
common among the Pueblo people
than those of the Plains, and the
Pueblo artist may have been influenced
by the Plains artist. This design,
representing rainbows and Kachina
beings, was painted by Homovi, who
worked for Jessie Walter Fewkes on
the preparation of his book, *Hopi
Katcinas,* 1903. Collected by Thomas V.
Keam, presented by Thea Heye.

175 Painted Hide Shield

Sioux. South Dakota, circa 1850
Diameter: 22¹/₄ inches   6/2195

The design portrays a fight between
Sioux and Crow warriors, some using
similar shields. Such shields were
considered to have a great medicinal
power. Often the central figure was the
owner.

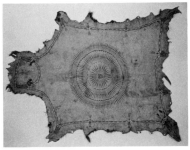

177

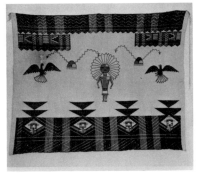

179

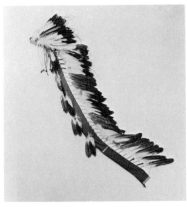

182

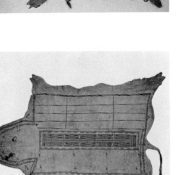

178

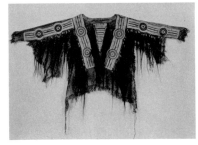

181

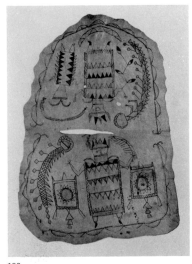

183

177 Painted Buffalo Hide
Teton Sioux. South Dakota, 1875-1890
73 x 97 inches   12/2158

An example of the sunburst motif, done with trader-supplied colors. Collected by George H. Bingenheimer.

178 Painted Cowhide
Sioux. South Dakota, 1880-1890
73 x 108 inches   10/2395

The box-and-border motif was painted with buffalo-bone brushes. Pressed against the surface of the hide, these produced the slightly indented effect. Such hides, painted and decorated by women, were used as garments.

179 Brocaded Cotton Shawl
Hopi Pueblo. Walpi, Arizona, 1900-1910
55 x 72 inches   6/6361

Worn for ceremonial occasions. The designs depict two eagles and Tawa, the Sun Kachina, in the center. Collected by George H. Pepper.

180 Painted Deer Hide   (see page 24)

181 Man's War Shirt
Brulé Sioux. Fort Laramie, South Dakota 1855
Length (open) 58 inches   17/6694

Obtained from the Brulé chief Spotted Tail (1833-81) when he surrendered in 1855. A magnificent example of an unusual quilling technique. Collected by Brigadier General Charles G. Sawtelle.

182 Feathered Bonnet
Cheyenne. Montana, circa 1880
Length: 80 inches   14/2242

This most familiar single object of the North American Indian culture may have originated among the Sioux. It was used only by the Plains people. Collected by General Nelson A. Miles. Presented by Mrs. Samuel K. Reber and Major Sherman Miles.

183 Painted Deerhide Medicine Shirt
Chiricahua Apache. Arizona
Circa 1880
Length: 47 inches   16/1349

The figures represent mythological beings. Collected by Major John G. Bourke, presented by his nieces, Mrs. Alexander H. Richardson and Mrs. Alexander W. Maish.

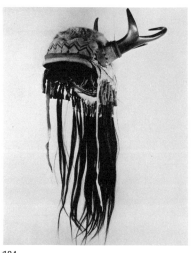

184

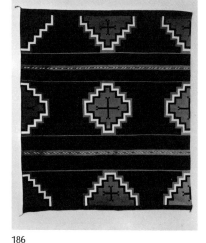

186

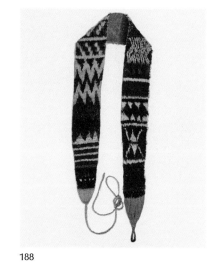

188

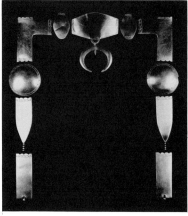

185

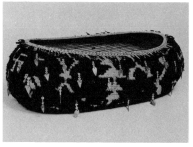

187

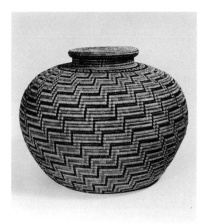

189

184 Antelope Headdress

Chiricahua Apache. Arizona
Circa 1900
Length: 25 inches   4/5072

Decorated with paint, fur, hair, and trade cloth, this headdress with antelope horns attached reflects the art of the Apache before it was influenced by outside contacts. Presented by Thea Heye.

185 Silver Bridle

Navajo. New Mexico, circa 1880
Length: 17¹⁄₂ inches   22/8176

Patterned after Spanish bridles of the period, this was made by Atsidi Chon, one of the first Navajo smiths. The decoration is incised or engraved with a file—a technique predating the use of stamped designs. Collected by Douglas G. Graham, U.S. Indian Agent, and presented by Evelyn B. Lent, G. B. Oman, Beatrice A. B. Young, and Mary F. B. VanHouten.

186 Woolen Blanket

Navajo. Ganado, Arizona, circa 1890
77 x 91 inches   22/9190

This unusually large, tightly woven piece is of the style influenced by Lorenzo Hubbell at Ganado. Collected in 1890 by Colonel Joseph T. Clarke.

187 Feather Canoe Basket

Pomo. California, circa 1900
24 x 61 inches   23/5700

The surface of the finely woven container is covered with wild canary and mallard-duck feathers. Small carved abalone and shell beads decorate the exterior. Baskets of such unusually large size were intended as gifts, or for the storage of especially valuable ceremonial objects. Collected by Judge Nathan Bijur, presented by Mr. and Mrs. Harry Bijur.

188 Feather Belt

Pomo. California, circa 1900
5¹⁄₂ x 68 inches   16/984

Such belts were considered to have the power to frighten enemies. This example, woven on a milkweed fiber base, to be worn across the shoulder, was made by Charles Benson. Presented by Thea Heye.

189 Globular Basket

Chumash. Santa Ynez, California
Circa 1800
9 x 11 inches   21/4783

Created in a coiled weave, with black and red design, this smoothly rounded container and cover is an early example of the superb basketry produced by Pacific Coast craftsmen.

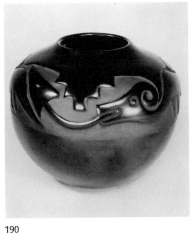

190

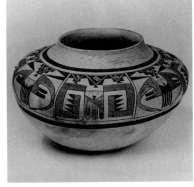

192

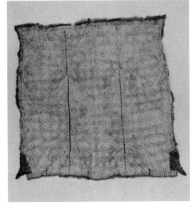

194

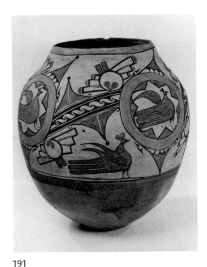

191

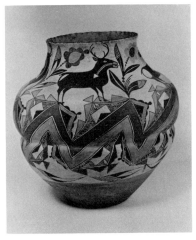

193

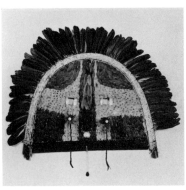

195

90 Carved Blackware Bowl
San Ildefonso Pueblo. New Mexico
1969
8½ x 11 inches   24/3223

This rotund vessel bears the Avanyu
design deeply carved into the surface.
It was made by Rose González, one
of today's outstanding pottery artists
of the Southwest. Presented by the
artist.

91 Polychrome Tinaja
Zia Pueblo. New Mexico, circa 1925
19 x 22 inches   16/5780

This painted storage jar is typical of
the older work from the Zia Pueblo.
The tinaja is larger than the more
commonly used olla. Made by Rosaria,
collected by John L. Nelson.

192 Polychrome Olla
Hopi Pueblo. Walpi, Arizona, circa 1900
9½ x 16 inches   16/8057

Typical of the squat globular bowls of
the Western Pueblo people, this
was made by Nampeyó of First Mesa.
Presented by the Philadelphia
Academy of Natural Sciences.

193 Polychrome Bowl
Acoma Pueblo. New Mexico
Circa 1900
13 x 13 inches   23/4992

The flare and the unusual treatment
of the waist of this beautifully painted
olla add to its graceful proportions.
Collected by Mrs. Prince Swift.

194 Painted Guanaco Hide
Tehuelche. Patagonia, Argentina
Circa 1915
62 x 64 inches   13/976

Such garments, once common in the
Tierra del Fuego region, have
disappeared along with the natives of
the region. Collected by Samuel K.
Lothrop.

195 Feather-Decorated Mask
Tapirapé. Goyaz, Brazil, circa 1960
29 x 43 inches   23/3299

Male dancers wear these huge Cara
Grande masks during the Banana
Festival ceremonies, when they appear
in pairs, representing the souls of
enemies killed in battle. Collected by
Borys Malkin.

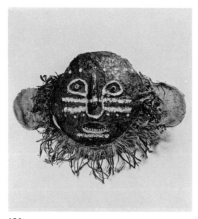

196

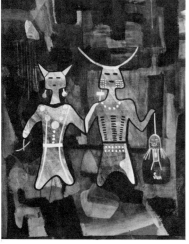

197

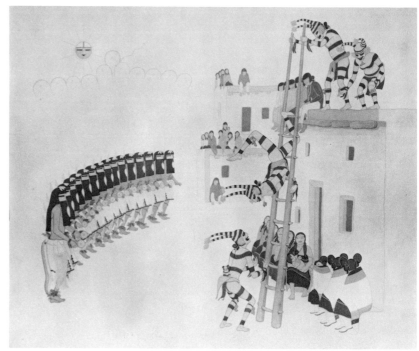

198

196 Bark Mask
Tukuna. São Paulo de Olivença, Brazil
Circa 1950
19 x 32 inches   24/7971

Representing Ama, the Storm Demon.
Such masks are worn by the ñöö
demons, dressed in bark cloth, who
appear in the Girls' Puberty Ceremony.
Collected by Harald Schultz.

197 Tempera Painting
San Ildefonso. New Mexico, 1964
16¹/₂ x 19¹/₂ inches   23/4133

The Marriage, by Joe V. Aguilar. This
abstract portrayal of a wedding
ceremony is an example of the
combination of early traditional and
more contemporary styles.

198 Watercolor Painting
Hopi Pueblo. Shungopovy, Arizona
Circa 1930
19 x 22¹/₄ inches   23/1268

The Delight Makers, by Fred Kabotie,
depicting the interlude between
Kachina Dance sets, when the clowns
perform antics. Presented by Charles
and Ruth deYoung Elkus.

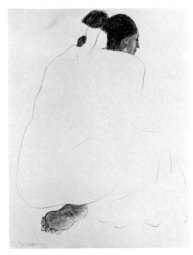

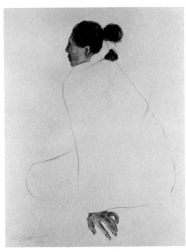

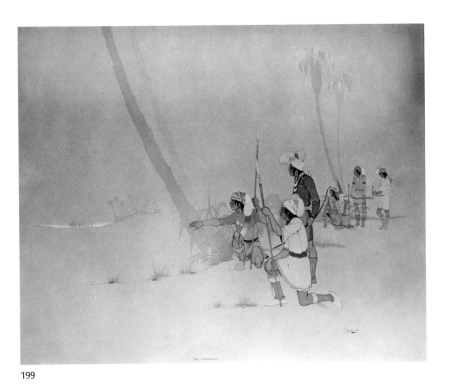

199

200

199 Watercolor Painting
Creek-Seminole. Oklahoma, 1966
16 x 20 inches   23/6992

The Intruders, by Jerome Tiger.
Seminole warriors view with
apprehension the approach of a group
of White men.

200 Oil Pastels   (on the covers)
Navajo. Chinle, Arizona, 1973
23 x 29 inches   24/8344

Navajo Woman, by R. C. Gorman,
one of the foremost of today's Indian
painters. His work embodies the
spirit of the past and captures that of
the present.

Women's dresses from tribes of western North America
1875-1925

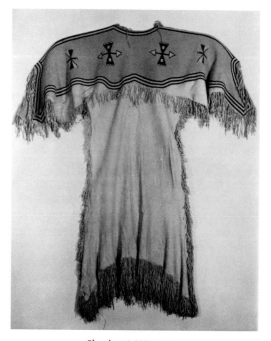

Shoshoni, Wyoming

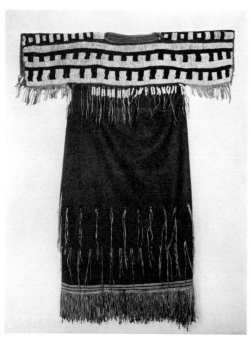

Blackfoot, Montana

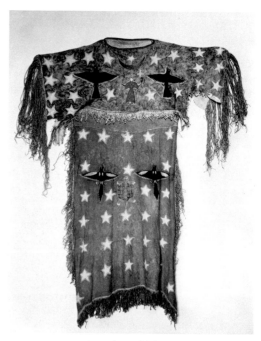

Arapaho, Oklahoma

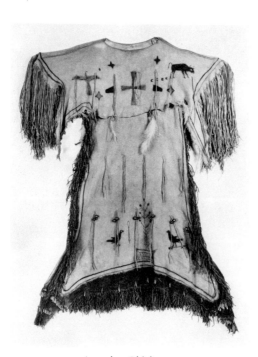

Arapaho, Oklahoma

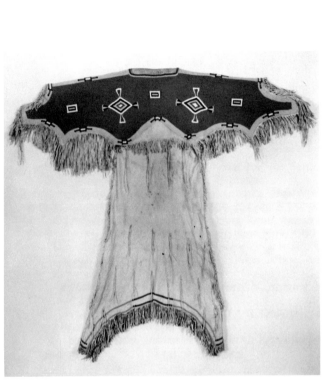

Brule Sioux, South Dakota

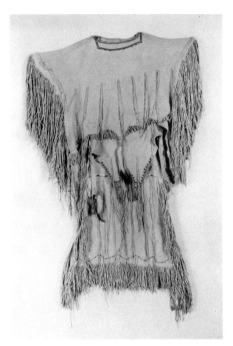

Kiowa, Oklahoma

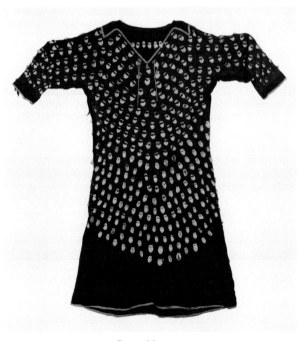

Crow, Montana

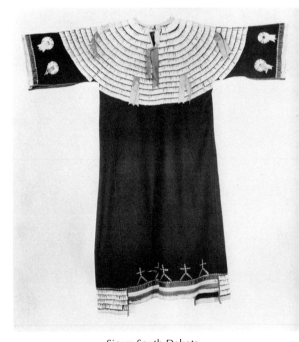

Sioux, South Dakota

RIT - WALLACE LIBRARY
CIRCULATING LIBRARY BOOKS

OVERDUE FINES AND FEES FOR <u>ALL</u> BORROWERS

* Recalled = $1/ day overdue (no grace period)
* Billed = $10.00/ item when returned 4 or more weeks overdue
* Lost Items = replacement cost+$10 fee
* All materials must be returned or renewed by the duedate.